machado:

A Dialogue with Time

machado:

A Dialogue with Time

Nature as an Expression of Temporality in the Poetry of Antonio Machado

Norma Louise Hutman

UNIVERSITY OF NEW MEXICO PRESS

Manufactured in the United States of America by
The University of New Mexico Printing Plant, Albuquerque.
Library of Congress Catalog Card No. 70-78554
First edition.

—FOR FLORENCE HUTMAN

how often referred to as my typist . . .

Acknowledgments

Portions of this study originally comprised a part of my doctoral dissertation presented to the University of Pittsburgh. To those responsible for the creation and award of the Andrew Mellon fellowships, to my dissertation committee, numberless librarians and one patient typist, I owe great appreciation for the completion of that initial work. I am particularly grateful to Dr. Hayward Keniston and Dr. Rupert Allen for their suggestions during the dissertation's preparation. My other obligations are those due my students and my many friends who are not Hispanists: my introduction to the Generation of '98 derives from courses prepared for the former while many of my translations were made for the latter.

Contents

A Note on Methods of Translation and Spanish Metrics

SPANISH POETRY, unlike English, is syllabic. While Spanish metrical practice recognizes the principal accent patterns of English—iambic, anapestic, trochaic, dactylic, and the amphibrach—their significance in most poems is slight and incidental. Only occasionally does a Spanish poet consistently cultivate marked rhythms throughout his work. José de Espronceda, the nineteenth-century romantic, exemplifies the repeated use of distinct accent patterns, while Machado wrote relatively few such poems.

The basic forms of Spanish metrics depend on the number of syllables in a line, not on the number of feet. The most common measures are the octosyllabic (with its origins in the twelfth-century epic and minstrel verse forms) and the hendecasyllabic (of Renaissance origin). Insofar as one accepts the theory that basic verse forms reflect the speech pattern of a language, the natural Spanish line contains 8 syllables, and the 11-syllable line, being a later and consciously stylistic innovation, is its aristocratic counterpart. Most sonnets (also of Renaissance origin) are hendecasyllabic; most dramatic verse (almost the entire Theatre of the Golden Age) is octosyllabic. Combinations of regular lines and their hemistichs are also common. In these cases the hemistich is called the *quebrado*—i.e., the broken part—and the style, *pie quebrado*. The *quebrado* of an 8-syllable line obviously has 4 syllables; but the *quebrados* of an 11-syllable line can have 7 or, less frequently, 5 syllables. Verse forms based on a line of 6, 7, 9, 12 (an intentionally elegant and rather unwieldy form predating the hendecasyllable in Spain) are also possible, as are forms based on 14 syllables (the Spanish alexandrine). "A orillas del Duero," Machado's most complete vision of Spain, employs the alexandrine.

Spanish poetry recognizes both assonant and consonant rhyme. Verse forms are traditionally divided into *arte mayor* (lines of 9 or more syllables) and *arte menor* (lines of 8 syllables or less). Both categories include examples of assonance and consonance, but consonant rhyme has been more common in *arte mayor* forms, until the cultivation of free verse.

Assonant rhyme is not readily perceptible to Anglo-Saxon ears because English verbal structure lacks an identical form for rendering rhyme schemes based entirely on vowels. For example, *sueños* rhymes with *le pego,* the assonance being in e, o; and with assonance in i, a: *en mi vida* rhymes with *este día.*

It was my original intention to translate all Machado's poetry as free verse because of the basic differences between verse structures in the two languages. However, I soon discovered that such translations were in no way indicative of the nature of the original poems. In order to convey even the paraphrasable content of Machado's work, I found it necessary to reproduce his original verse forms as closely as possible. Therefore, I have established a few rather general principles:

1) I have endeavored not to move words from one line to another. Instead I have tried, as far as possible, to retain the original content of each verse. (There are about 12 exceptions to this principle in all of the texts translated.)
2) Each Spanish verse form is rendered in a comparable English

pattern, so that octosyllables usually become iambic tetrameter or anapestic tetrameter. To provide a corresponding structure, the one alexandrine has been reproduced in an abnormally long English verse line; hemistichs (*pie quebrado*) remain English hemistichs, etc.

3) Where the rhyme is consonantal the rhyme scheme of the original poem has been retained in English; assonance has been translated as free verse and I have sought to retain some fidelity to the accent patterns of the original.

4) The use of enjambment in the translations is proportional to its use in those of Machado's poems quoted here. But no effort has been made in every poem to match each instance in Spanish by a similar one in English.

In general, then, this is a translation of meanings, not of words. You cannot have both, at least in equal degree, since English and Spanish are but slightly kindred tongues. Despite the facility with which, for example, words terminating in "-tion" yield Spanish "-ción," and vice versa, actual translation is thereby only slightly aided. For ideas have no declensions or endings whereby they may be recognized and fitted into an alien language. Successful translation creates a kindred idea, a complementary poem, with its own integrity and its own uniqueness. As a translation it is not the same work of art, and its success is its own business, at best only partially but recognizably related to the work it hopes to recreate. If a translation attains a measure of greatness, it does so, paradoxically, on its own. For in the translated poem, the poet's own work does not survive; only its distorted reflection remains.

I have undertaken to translate Machado's poems in the face of my own obvious misgivings, because no matter whose translation I might use, I would carp and decry its failures and limitations. And one might better carp at one's own shortcomings.

The Generation of 1898: An Introduction

IN 1898 the American navy annihilated the Spanish fleet in Manila Bay; in defeat Spain would shortly recognize the end of her empire in the Western Hemisphere. A proud people, the Spanish had predicted victory, for the Armada of 1898, no more invincible than the *Armada Invencible* of 1588, was part of a national myth. But when that myth was destroyed by the ships of a relatively new nation in a distant harbor, Spain responded to defeat by shrugging her shoulders and, having read of the battle in the Sunday press, went to the bullrings that same afternoon.

Thus Andrés Hurtado, protagonist of Pío Baroja's *El árbol de la ciencia* (*The Tree of Knowledge*), paints the Madrid—indeed, the Spain—of 1898. His is the voice of a literary generation, the Generation of '98, whose intellectual formation is to be found in the nineteeth century but whose voice and vision are part of the twentieth. Andrés embodies his age as don Juan epitomizes one facet of nineteenth-century romanticism or as Il Cortegiano reflects the Renaissance. A romantic born out of time, he dreams and destroys himself even as the age he represents emerges, searches, dreams and burns out. Equally representative spokesmen might be Angel Ganivet's Pío Cid, Unamuno's Augusto Pérez, Azorín's autobiographical "little philosopher" and, indeed, Machado's "traveler in dreams upon a harsh road": each fictional protagonist embodying the roles of individual, dreamer, wanderer, and quixotic idealist.

There is some disagreement concerning whom one ought include in the Generation. But, with the possible addition of Ramón María del Valle-Inclán, these are its principal figures: Angel Ganivet y García, Miguel de Unamuno y Jugo, Antonio Machado y Ruiz, Pío Baroja y Nessi, and José Martínez Ruiz, called Azorín.[1] Born at the end of an age of political pettiness destined to terminate in civil war, the Generation of '98 was an oasis of uncompromising ideals and ideas.

The controversy which has surrounded a definition of the Generation of '98, its membership, and even the validity of the term "generation," derives partly from the attitudes of the writers involved. Although the name was coined for himself and his contemporaries by Azorín, his fellow writers were so essentially individualistic that each tended to reject the definition and to regard himself as unique, the member of no school, movement or generation. Most articulate in his objection was Pío Baroja, who decried the existence of a Generation of '98, then added that if such a thing existed, he was not part of it.[2] Yet today, discounting the prejudices and protests of some of the writers themselves and using ideology rather than chronology as a guide, we can rather easily define the Generation, describe its debt to and alienation from its own cultural past, and characterize each prominent figure in the movement.

Rooted in philosophy, the Generation is an ideological rather than a historic fact. Ganivet, for example, who shows both the influence of and alienation from prevailing literary concepts, is most often seen as a precursor. More accurately, he articulates the fundamental questions that are posed in various forms by the rest of the Generation. His treatment of truth and interpretation in *El escultor de su alma,* for example, finds a spiritual counterpart in Unamuno's short novel, *San Manuel Bueno, mártir.* Separated by thirty-three years, these works of Ganivet and Unamuno nonetheless share a single vision of life, a vision to which the objectivity preached by French realism was alien. For the Generation there was no objectivity. Objectivity represents a desire to portray truth and from the beginning, as Machado was to say, doubt was the only possible absolute. They were selective traditionalists believing that one must take from tradition, as Ganivet declares, the only thing it can really offer: spirit. Without exception they embraced don Quijote, the symbol and spirit of an irrational ideal, but not Cervantes, baroque art or even the stylistic majesty of the *Quijote.* For them the mad don was a man, not a literary classic. They took over Calderón's "life is a dream" and Manrique's famous lines—"Life is a river / which goes to the sea / that is death"—but for the playwright's doctrines or the poet's moralizing they had neither time nor interest.

With Leopoldo Alas, not too accurately styled a Spanish naturalist, they felt the reality of place, the collective psychology of towns and cities. Azorín's city of Yecla is personified like Alas' Vetusta but without the ironic humor that represents "the heroic city taking its siesta."[3] Galdós evokes Toledo in the novel *Angel Guerra* and Madrid in *Fortunata y Jacinta* in a manner which Baroja will reflect in, respectively, *Camino de perfección* and *El árbol de la ciencia.*

Concern for the nation, particularly in the attitude Baroja calls "bitter patriotism," is not new with the Generation. An obvious spiritual precursor is the anguish at human slaughter—"for a king and a cause they did not know"[4]—portrayed in Alas' "Adios, *cordera.*" The conflict between tradition and progress, with decided religious and anticlerical elements—as represented in the late nineteenth century by Alas, Pérez Galdós, Alarcón, Blasco Ibáñez and Pardo Bazán—is essentially the conflict of Machado's "Spain that desires to be born / between one Spain that prays / and another which yawns."[5]

The Generation also sought to articulate in art those conflicts which are waged within an individual. The concern with psychological aberration, which pervades Galdós' *La sombra, Angel Guerra* and the figure of Maxí in *Fortunata y Jacinta*, reappears in the obsession with liberty portrayed by Ganivet in *El escultor de su alma,* in Unamuno's treatment of jealousy in *Abel Sánchez,* in Baroja's protagonists who seek knowledge of themselves, and in Azorín's heroes haunted by time and place. Galdós' representation of Angel Guerra who conquers his obsession only in his death anticipates the ironic victory which Baroja describes for Andrés Hurtado, ennobled by his suicide.

The concept of religion as an active dedication rather than a cult, espoused by Unamuno in his essays and climaxed in *San Manuel Bueno*, does not differ radically from that envisioned by Galdós in *Angel Guerra* (in the person of Leré), *Nazarín*, *Halma* and *Misericordia.* As the romantics of the 1830's were educated in the classic tradition, the Generation had obviously gone to school in the nineteenth century, although, in the fashion of all romantics, they were given to proclaiming their own originality.[6] Skeptical romantics who doubted the existence of absolute truths, they were nevertheless absolutists in their loyalties. One must question, seek, doubt, encourage questioning and seeking in others; one must create an ideal, then serve it, and even, if necessary, die for it. Such dedication does not recognize compromise. Uncertainty is a facet of the ideal's nature and a measure of its dignity. Unamuno praises don Quijote: "He fought for Dulcinea who did not exist."

Greatness is measured by the extent of the dedication and the nobility of the goal, not by any standards of reality or validity.

Thus it is no surprise that, in addition to don Quijote, Unamuno's spiritual ancestors included Spinoza, Kierkegaard and Pascal.

Until recently it has been considered rather heretical to call this romanticism. Only Professor F. Courtney Tarr's 1925 monograph "Romanticism in Spain and Spanish Romanticism" bore early witness to the romantic character of the Generation.[7] Certainly Spain had its formal romanticism in the first half of the nineteenth century, a romanticism imported by writers with a classical orientation whose political exile occasioned their exposure to French and English romanticism. Inspired by the novels of Walter Scott, *Hernani* and the poems of Byron and Shelley, these classicists returned to Spain determined to be romantics. Some of their work predictably lacks spontaneity. But the Generation was not particularly fond of formal Spanish romanticism and made exception principally of the emotional world-view of Espronceda, the fragile melancholy of Bécquer and, above all, the skeptical essays of Larra.[8] And all three are indicative of the Generation's point of departure.

More than any other romantic, Larra foreshadows the Generation: biting social satire, universality of interest, concern for and, more important, participation in the experience of suffering. Larra places himself in the midst of the holocaust and feels the earth slip beneath his feet. In his suicide, as in his concern for Spain, he prefigures Ganivet. Larra's bitter sense of unfulfilled time passing, of human impotence in the face of tasks to be done, of life wasted and death stalking are reiterated in Machado's dialogue with time and in Azorín's stark comment: "this feeling, that it is always late, has been the central concept of my life."[9]

Yet Larra is a relatively remote ancestor. The most obvious and immediate influences are neither Spanish nor primarily literary, for the mind of the Generation was shaped largely by Leibniz, Spinoza, Kant, Schopenhauer, Kierkegaard, Nietzsche,

Bergson and Heidegger. Even the German philosopher Krause, rejected early by the Generation, played his role, for *krausismo* directed Spanish writers toward Germany and the continent in general, gave them new models, and opened the doors of Spanish metaphysics, not for the universities but for the poets and novelists, who thus became the intellectual elite of an intellectually bankrupt nation.

The most prominent philosophic influences are easily discernible in specific authors. Ganivet's Pío Cid is a fairly faithful descendent of Zarathustra, and Azorín domesticates rather than alters the myth of the eternal return. Pío Cid withdraws to the top floor of a boarding house, not to the heights, although his motives are Zarathustra's; the cycles of Azorín's world are the repetitive rhythms of village life and the humbler processes of nature. In his adaptations, Unamuno is more willful. He is closest to Pascal whose statements on faith, reason and ultimate uncertainty he recalls. In Spinoza's *Ethics* he finds, implicitly, his own concern for the tension between reason and desire, since he cannot reconcile Spinoza's definition of essence as "the effort with which each thing endeavors to survive in its being" with the philosopher's subsequent dismissal of belief in personal immortality. Seizing upon Spinoza's characterization of such belief as an absurdity not meriting refutation, Unamuno equates this refusal to offer a refutation with his tragic sense of life: "the vital skepticism which derives from the collision of reason and desire . . . from [which] is born the holy, the beloved, the saving uncertainty, our supreme consolation."[10] In Kierkegaard's definition of an anguished faith and in Kant's critique of reason, Unamuno also seeks positions similar to his own. Baroja is, by contrast, quite content with what he finds in Schopenhauer, under whose deterministic world will his characters labor.

Machado adapts less than Unamuno but accepts his sources less enthusiastically than Baroja. First introduced to a time-oriented philosophy while studying with Bergson, he subsequently tended to embrace philosophers in accord with the degree to which their concerns paralleled his own. In discovering Heidegger, some years before the rest of Spain, he found an ontological explanation of man which included past, present and future. Heidegger's inclusive time, his definition of *Dasein* as containing time past and time to be (conceived as one temporal reality), and his emphasis on human finitude provide a philosophic parallel to Machado's poetic vision. Finally, Azorín directly transferred Nietzsche's myth of the eternal return to those novels from which he sought to excise plot, action, characters and time.

If the intellectual climate of Spain at the end of the nineteenth century would not seem generally ready for these writers, there were nevertheless certain liberal elements at work in the traditionally church-oriented, ultra-conservative schools. With the founding of the Instituto Libre de Enseñanza, Francisco Giner de los Ríos initiated an independent, freethinking educational concept in a nation where independence in education as well as thought was regarded as radical and dangerous. For some of the liberals of his day, Giner and his school were symbols; for others, personal influences. Machado, whose elegy for his dead teacher has survived the Instituto itself, was one for whom Giner was both.

Just as it is impossible to simplify the nature of the Generation, so it is pointless to draw up a list of sources, themes, experiences and educational factors which apply to all its members. Before considering each author we can, however, write two words which characterize the Generation: one is "I" and the other "Spain." Any study of the nation supposes a prior study of the self, for the ideal Spaniard who will build the Spain of the Generation's dream is himself something of a dream: free, Nietzschean, a modern don Quijote.

This "I" with which the Generation is concerned is a time-haunted self, a skeptic, a seeker, sometimes an adventurer (literally and figuratively) but sometimes also an observer of life, a man unsure of what he seeks, and a man preoccupied with death.

So frequently does a protagonist speak for his creator that the Generation confuses individual identity. Both Pío Cid and Pedro Mártir are idealized recreations and spokesmen of their author, Ganivet, and their philosophies are his. Unamuno, always elusive, nevertheless gives us glimpses of himself in two protagonists, Augusto Pérez and Joaquín Monegro, and more distorted impressions in other characters, especially in his skeptical priest, Manuel Bueno. Baroja, always outspoken, draws a number of self-portraits in his novels. Baroja's name can be substituted for the name of many of his heroes, but the most autobiographical protagonist whom he offers us is Andrés Hurtado. José Martínez Ruiz is so completely identical with his fictional counterpart, Antonio Azorín, that he eventually takes his protagonist's name. In any study of the Generation, critics understandably tend to use author and protagonist as synonyms. Because the fictional counterpart tends to fulfill the author's ideology better than the author himself, such identifications can be dangerous. When some qualifications are made, however, we can safely take the fictional philosophy of life and the fate of the hero as reflections of the goals and failures of the artist. The Generation thus tends to wear a very thin mask in fictional works.

In addition, the Generation's ideal of Spain is closely associated with its protagonist, for the nation and particularly the landscape are intimately related to the man who dwells in that landscape. Both Ganivet and Unamuno constructed theories on the compatibility of land and inhabitant. In their evocation of place —towns, deserted mesetas, mountains, houses—Azorín and Baroja exemplified the theory, and Machado expressed its essence when he wrote: "Sad lands, lands so sad as to have a soul."

The Spain of the Generation is a spiritual cripple, sad but haughty, as barren of soul as of soil. Dry, rocky Castile becomes the visible counterpart of a violated past and a sterile present. The provincial towns are touchstones for theories of stagnation, intolerance and provincialism. And the castles in ruin are evocations of past glories and idle dreams.

For man, past and future play vital roles in the nation's life: Spain recollected, Spain observed, Spain dreamed. And in the end the same hero is needed to redeem the nation as is required to redeem human nature: a man beyond reason, author of his own ideals, free because his security lies within him. The Generation has many protagonists and the yardstick against which they are measured is an antirational one: don Quijote, a timeless figure fitted to a new context in a new time.

The first of the Generation's major figures chronologically, Angel Ganivet has proven to be one of Spain's more elusive intellectuals. For example, Ganivet's satire on the techniques of realism stands in paradoxical juxtaposition to those practices which he shares with the novelists of the late nineteenth century. In a letter to his friend Rafael Gago, Ganivet comments that part of *Los trabajos del infatigable creador Pío Cid* was written to mock excess description and the unnecessary multiplication of detail in realist novels,[11] but he himself employs copious details in order to characterize. More specifically he has the narrator of *Los trabajos* denounce those who study a man's life as you would study a laboratory animal.[12] His affinity is rather with Pérez Galdós and with all those nineteenth-century writers who are capable of forgiving man his folly and comprehending him rather than dissecting him.

Ultimately, however, it is not so much theme as technique which relates Ganivet to the nineteenth century and which describes his role as a mediator between realism and the Generation. Ganivet uses the realist social structure to create both the primitive world of Maya (*La conquista del reino de Maya por el último conquistador español Pío Cid*) and the universal world of *Los trabajos*. The social structure of Baroja's novels and the function of the town as a personage in Unamuno's *San Manuel Bueno* are also similar.

Not unlike the image of the grotto in Galdós *El abuelo*, where landscape fuses with the symbolic echo of the two voices, is the cave in *El escultor*, which is both an evocation of Granada and one facet of the light-darkness imagery dominating the play. A similar role will be played by the images of lake and mountain in Unamuno's *Abel Sánchez* and by the poor towns of Castile which are both landscape and soulscape in the novels and short stories of Azorín.

Finally, the oft cited use of symbolic or overtly significant names in Galdós' works—Nazarín, Halma (*alma*—soul), Benigna, Torquemada, los Babel—also figures in Ganivet's novels. Pío Cid is, for example, a pious (*pío*) hero, the first half of his name suggesting the role of high priest which he plays in the kingdom of Maya and the latter half his role as national hero. In *El escultor*, Pedro Mártir is not only one who dies for freedom; he also bears the name of the street on which Ganivet was born, linking the play intimately with Granada and evoking the theme of return, dominant in the last act. The sculptor's daughter is named Alma as is the Duchess in *Los trabajos*, whose full name is Soledad de Almadura (loneliness of a hard soul). Even names such as Cecilia, named for the patroness of Granada, and Martina, whose name derives from *martillo* (hammer), are significant in a manner reminiscent of Galdós.

This same penchant for symbolic names appears in those works of Unamuno and Baroja which bear the closest thematic relationship to Ganivet. In *San Manuel Bueno*, Unamuno's protagonist bears the Spanish equivalent of the name Emmanuel, while the man who joins his cause, and is reborn thereby, is named Lázaro and his sister is called Angela. Baroja names the hero of his satire on colonialism Silvester Paradox and his political reformer César. Unamuno's version of the Cain and Abel tale and even Machado's invention of a name for his secret love, Guiomar, are similar instances.[13]

Ganivet obviously took over many of the fictional principles of the nineteenth century without necessarily subscribing to all its tenets. The issue is further complicated by the brevity of his career. A suicide at 33, he did not live long enough to participate in the literary scene of the 1920's and 1930's. Too close to the Generation for proper perspective, Ganivet's critics have tended to overemphasize the temporal gap. Except for Doris King Arjona's brilliant and still valid essay, "*Voluntad* and *Abulia* in Contemporary Spanish Literature,"[14] Ganivet has rarely been placed in his proper context. Happily, his centenary, observed in 1965, revealed a more balanced if still incomplete reevaluation of this complex writer.[15]

Critical overemphasis on the essay *Idearium español*, which interprets Spanish history, potential and weaknesses,[16] has also tended to obscure the significance of Ganivet's ideology in establishing the basic preoccupations of the entire Generation.

Simply stated, Ganivet believed that man is inherently perfectable—although certainly not perfect—and that his task as man is to perfect himself.[17] In this way the protagonists of Ganivet's novels and play resemble Zarathustra, and the vision they strive to fulfill is indeed a concept of the superman. But man cannot accomplish this end in a single lifetime.

In a critical passage of the *Idearium*, Ganivet explains man's relationship to the ideas he produces:

> Fruit comes from a flower but it belongs not to the flower but to the tree. Man is the flowering of his species and the ideas he creates be-

long not to him but to the species which nurtures and preserves them.[18]

Similar themes appear in *Los trabajos,* a short story called "The Ruins of Granada," and the play *El escultor* which derives from that story. But the key sentence is articulated in the *Idearium*: "I believe that it is the idea alone which truly lives."[19] Thus reality, for Ganivet, is ultimately transformed by ideas.

If this statement is regarded as central both to the essay and to Ganivet's thought, some conclusions are immediately forthcoming. First, Ganivet has set the tone for the Generation by subordinating all practical considerations to ideology; also, his work constitutes a synthesized whole in which the bold affirmation of the *Idearium* is fulfilled in the symbolic death which concludes *El escultor*.

Ganivet subordinates all his works and all other concerns to the development of this theme. Demanding synthesis and logic in others, he imposes essential unity on his own work. His single-minded dedication to the revitalization of Spain and the instruction of his friends recalls Pío Cid's affirmation in *La conquista*: "If our ideals do not inspire us to sacrifice our lives, they are not worth the effort of propagandizing in their behalf nor of imposing them on others."[20] Sick, exhausted, literally worn out at 33, Ganivet satisfied his own requirement. His suicide is also an ironic fulfillment of his words on man and the ideas man produces for humanity. The *Idearium's* key passage reads in full:

> I see no great difference between life and death, for I believe that it is the idea alone which truly lives. But the individual too must live, for he creates ideas, as must the species which preserve them. Thus I would not concede any particular importance to death and less to the manner in which one dies. What saddens me is the recognition that in the death of the body also perish all present and future creations of the spirit.[21]

Ganivet articulated an idea which perhaps no longer needs its author, although the age which followed, lost in the *abulia* or lack of will which he described and named, showed a need for the powers of insight and synthesis which perished with him.

The synthesis is first embodied in Ganivet's fiction in the character of Pío Cid. But Pío is also human, and subject as he is to fate and death, remains less than the ideal protagonist, less than the Nietzschean ideal. Thus in the first of his novels Ganivet gives Pío Cid a second identity. Lost in central Africa, Pío stumbles on a hidden civilization—he literally bumps into it after mounting a domesticated hippopotamus—where he assumes the identity of a long absent high priest or Igana Iguru called Arimi.

Arimi is "he of the mysterious death," a name which acquires additional symbolic value in *Los trabajos.* In *La conquista,* Pío uses this identity to change the customs and beliefs of the people. Thus Arimi is also the man of will, the man of action, resembling both the conquistadores and don Quijote. The transformation of Arimi into an idea is completed in *Los trabajos,* in which Pío pronounces a discourse on "the man of will." This speech is based an on acrostic derived from the name Arimi:

A-rtis initium dolor.
R-atio initium erroris.
I-nitium sapientae vanitas.
M-ortis initium amor.
I-nitium vitae libertas.[22]

Taken together this acrostic and Pío's extensive commentary on it form a resumé of Ganivet's thought and an outline of the Generation's major themes.

That from sorrow springs creativity (*Artis initium dolor*—Sorrow is the beginning of art) is hardly a new theory. But the role of suffering is particularly significant to the Generation, which sees creativity as the essential human activity. To perfect oneself is a creative act, a kind of artistic endeavor and, as an artistic expression, it is rooted in grief. Early in *Los trabajos*, Ganivet dismisses happiness in unequivocal terms:

I scarely concede happiness any great importance. It is an aspect of life but not its essence. For what is gained if some fool is loved by a woman whose love makes him happy, if his foolishness is a disgrace to his humanity? And what is lost if a man of genius lives always in loneliness and grief if these inspire noble endeavors in him which in turn enrich the humanity offended by a happy fool?[23]

This emphasis on the inherent dignity of man, manifested by the artist and offended by the fool, suggests that human worth is inherent (*Initium sapientiae vanitas*—Vanity is the beginning of wisdom). Ganivet has no more patience with academic rationalization than with happy fools (*Ratio initium erroris*—Reason is the beginning of error). The deification of reason is as harshly denounced by Unamuno, Baroja and Machado.

Reason is not, however, man's only enemy. His inherent dignity is constantly pitted against forces which seek to enslave his individuality. Love is a perennial trap; death, fate's ultimate victory. Only in freedom from love, declares Ganivet, is ultimate creativity realized; only in freedom from death, absolute freedom.

Pursuing the object of his passion man is distracted from his proper end, the perfection of self. Pío does not rule out love for everyone; rather he sees in the sacrificing of love a greater good. In the last lines of his discourse, Pío, commenting on the redemption of a fallen woman, observes: "But one can do more than redeem her through love; one can rise still higher. . . ." But the discourse ends in mid-sentence.

What one can do is clear in the conclusion of *Los trabajos*, throughout *El escultor*, in Unamuno's *San Manuel Bueno*, Azorín's *El escritor*, and Machado's more anguished poems on the death of his wife: one can sacrifice love or accept its loss. Pío Cid leaves the Duchess Soledad because he knows only a human love for her. Pedro Mártir, the sculptor, sacrifices first his wife and then his passion for Alma, whom he does not immediately recognize as his daughter. In this final sacrifice, Pédro both frees himself from the slavery of love and fulfills the acrostic's next proposition (*Mortis initium amor*—Love is the beginning of death).

Alma dies and is symbolically transformed into a statue. Since she is Pedro's daughter and soul (the meaning of her name), she becomes now, in apotheosis, the creation of his will, and, as a statue, his artistic creation. She becomes an idea, symbolically immortal, given eternal life (*Initium vitae libertas*—Liberty is the beginning of life) by the artist who has given her form and existence. As Pedro's soul made immortal Alma immortalizes him and frees him from death.

Ganivet is able to communicate this final aspect of his theory only symbolically. Throughout his works immortality has been symbolized in stone: statues, the towers of the Alhambra, the ruins of Granada. If life is illusion—and because it is transient it must be unreal—then life must be transcended. If death is fate's ultimate victory, one must overcome death. In human as opposed to symbolic terms the only victory man can enjoy over the inevitability of death is found in choosing death, in suicide. Man transcends death by electing death. Arimi incarnates an ideal only because he is dead; Alma, offspring and creation of Pedro Mártir, immortalizes the soul only by her death and transformation into stone. Both Arimi and Alma are ideas: Arimi becomes an acrostic; Alma, a statue. Both thus become forms bestowing permanence upon fragile, perishable flesh and doomed humanity.

Literally read, this remains a doctrine of cold consolations. Yet, ironically, Ganivet is the Generation's consummate optimist. For Spain he envisions potential greatness; for man potential perfection. All his concepts are expressed in terms of affirmation. Even his theory of death is presented as liberation; suicide, as victory over fate. As the poet who sees in the ruins of Granada "not a petrification of life but another form of life,"[24] Ganivet sees a rebirth in all negation, all doubt and all apparent defeat. At the outset of an age of skepticism, he manages, with Nietzsche, to say "yea" in the face of despair. For to affirm, to be free, to be: these are acts of the will. And for Ganivet all truth is grounded in human volition.

Unamuno shares Ganivet's uncompromising devotion to difficult concepts and Ganivet's willingness to treat life in the light of uncertainty and death. But Unamuno's affirmations are different; doubt and the desire for immortality are Unamuno's absolutes, less fatal than those of Ganivet and yet no less final. For doubt and desire create only anguish and few have the courage, which Unamuno possessed, to turn despair into affirmation.

During a long, productive lifetime, Unamuno wrote countless essays, several short novels, plays both original and adapted from Greek and Latin dramas, three long novels—*Paz en la guerra (Peace in War)*, *Abel Sánchez* and *Niebla (Mist)*—and a few major essays. His principal works, in addition to some of the brief essays, are usually considered to be *Abel Sánchez, Niebla, San Manuel Bueno, mártir* (a short novel), *La vida de don Quijote y Sancho* and *Del sentimiento trágico de la vida (The Tragic Sense of Life)*.

Concerned with the nature of literature, Hispanic reality, professional philosophic discussion and almost every issue raised by philosophy, Unamuno's work is unified by an absence of dogma and by a personal, almost egocentric orientation. Philosophy, says Unamuno, does not exist; only philosophers exist, and out of their anguish, their personal despair, hope and rationalization, arise what we wrongly call philosophic systems. He maintains that only the individual is real. He despises humanity but calls each human being a world and a philosophy.

With this highly personal basis, the central tenet of Unamuno's thought quite naturally becomes the existential self. For don Miguel was a self-proclaimed egotist who anticipated the charge of damned pride by making such pride a virtue.[25] The passage which affirms his concern with pride characterizes his tragic sense of life: "It is better to live in pain [i.e., in hell] than in peace to cease to be."

The tragic sense of life is man's desire for immortality, existing at the same time as his realization that he cannot rationally prove his immortality. To accept on faith is to humble oneself before an acknowledged mystery and this Unamuno refuses to do. To despair is to make reason ultimate, ruling out all that reason cannot provide, but Unamuno dares man to be antirational, for reason establishes no ultimate answers and promises no ultimate wisdom. "This our longing never to die," he writes, paraphrasing Spinoza, "is our human essence."[26] His absolutism is of a personal and intense nature. In a passage central to the *Tragic Sense,* the philosopher expresses the human situation:

> I do not wish to die, no; nor do I wish so to desire. I want to live forever, forever, forever . . . this I, this poor self that I am and that I know myself to be here and now, and for this reason am I tortured by the question of the soul's immortality . . . of the immortality of this my soul . . . my own soul.[27]

All of don Miguel's work is colored by this unfulfilled desire. There are no answers: everything is simultaneously uncompromising and, paradoxically, arbitrary. We know nothing, but we must assert the value of our personal truth, just as that prototype of idealistic madmen, don Quijote, served his own subjective absolute. We are sure of nothing, but we must live creatively with our uncertainty. Unamuno's tenets are more than a paradox. For Unamuno, truth and reality are themselves paradoxical: unprovable and necessary, subjective and final, the source of our despair and the only support for our irrational hope.

Don Quijote, the Knight of the Woeful Figure, personifies this apparent contradiction. For don Quijote, as Unamuno portrays him, sees his own folly and, by confronting it, affirms the absurd. In Cervantes' hero the juxtaposition of doubt and affirmation are already present. "Never," Unamuno writes in *La Vida de don Quijote y Sancho,* "does don Quijote appear greater to us than in those moments in which he imposes his faith on those who would ridicule him and inspires them to defend furiously his ideals and to suffer for them."[28] This is the man of action, as Unamuno conceives him and would have us imitate him. The end of his struggle, like its motive, is uncertain—at best, each man's individual effort to transform reality.

More drastic than Ganivet, who believes at least in human dignity, and more dynamic than Machado, who is moved by doubt to search rather than to struggle, Unamuno makes a doctrine of doubt and affirms anguished uncertainty. In the age of political and personal disintegration which Ganivet portrayed in his essays, in a nation given to hollow pride and obsessed with the past, in a skeptical era, Unamuno incarnates the Spain of intellectual ferment, subjective hope and national crisis. As Salvador de Madariaga observes: "that he is great enough to bear this incarnation is a sufficient measure of his greatness."

Unamuno maintains that man has three selves: the man as others see him, the man as he would have himself seen, and the man as he is. Others tend to see in Unamuno the message they seek. And the real Unamuno? The real Unamuno speaks through questions and paradoxical images to say: "Agitar es algo" (It is some accomplishment to stir men up, to make them think).[29]

Within this context of doubt and man's unsatisfiable desire

for immortality, Unamuno addresses himself to specific problems in each of his works. Frustrated maternity is the subject of *La tía Tula,* while irrational creativity in a world dedicated to tangible truths comprises elements of *La vida de don Quijote.* More complex are the issues faced in *Abel Sánchez, Niebla, San Manuel Bueno* and *The Tragic Sense.* Chronology is of some use to the reader, not in establishing a progression in Unamuno's thought, but in discerning his repeated refusal to posit anything which he does not later contradict. *Nada menos que todo un hombre (Nothing Less than a Man)* affirms love. Yet this work is followed by *Abel Sánchez,* wherein envy begets death and the protagonist finds himself incapable of love. *El Cristo de Velázquez* evokes a personal, cosmic Christ but is followed by *San Manuel Bueno,* the tale of a priest without faith, who yet inspires faith in others, and eventually becomes a martyr to the paradox of himself.

Abel Sánchez juxtaposes two visions of life: "All hatred is envy" and "Each man is, as Job, the offspring of contradiction."[30] The first statement is easily documented in the novel by the two young men who find success in their respective fields: Joaquín (Cain) as a doctor and Abel as an artist. Yet Joaquín is jealous of Abel's facile and public triumph: popularity, fame and the woman Joaquín wished to marry become Abel's without effort. Paradoxically it is Joaquín's speech, interpreting and praising Abel's major painting, which lifts his friend and rival to artistic renown. Unconscious of his effect on Joaquín, Abel is truly the superficial man. But Joaquín does not recognize this. Rather he ceases to work and denies both his ability to love and his capacity to receive love. Ultimately, as in the biblical tale of Cain and Abel, Joaquín causes Abel's death, slaying himself in this final, irrevocable surrender to his pursuing devil.

However controversial the thesis that all hatred is grounded in envy, this is not the essential premise of the novel. For the deadly irony of Unamuno's portrait lies in the superiority of Joaquín to Abel. Joaquín first slays himself, metaphorically, in allowing his unfounded envy to devour him. The death of Abel is a lesser tragedy. The significant tragedy which Unamuno paints lies with the Faustian pawning of Joaquín's soul as it pursues and desires the superficial fame of Abel. If Joaquín and Abel are seen as two facets of a single soul, or as dual faces of man, then Joaquín's self-destruction reveals that the noble and the mediocre in man, his essence and his mask, can never fuse. Instead, man declares war on himself, so that the entire novel documents Unamuno's pronouncement, "Every man is the offspring of contradiction."

In novels more obviously ideological and symbolic, *Niebla* and *San Manuel Bueno,* Unamuno again examines the conflict inherent in being human. In the first of these novels, Unamuno obscures the traditional boundaries between author and protagonist in order to involve both in the tension described. For this new relationship don Miguel has a new name: he does not call *Niebla* a novel *(novela)* but a *nivola,* in which the world of the novel and that of its author collide and interact.

The interaction is most apparent when the protagonist refuses to die. Long disposed to suicide, Augusto Pérez decides suddenly that he wishes to live even as his author, Unamuno, enters the novel to serve his death notice. But the protagonist rejects the verdict of his creator. In turn, Unamuno declares to Augusto that as a fictional character in a novel he is merely an idea, a dream in the mind of his creator, subject to extinction on the author's whim. How then, Augusto replies, does the author know himself to be more than an idea in another mind, briefly real in another's dream, subject to ultimate extinction, powerless to prevent his own annihilation? Augusto dies, but the question persists, the doubt which erodes all certainty, corrupting equally reason and emotion.

In the last of his major fictional works, Unamuno treats directly the theme of creativity and radical doubt. For Manuel Bueno, the priest, believes nothing. But for the good of the people, who, as he tells one confidant, Lázaro, could not live with the truth, unknown and perhaps too terrible to be known,[31] he pretends to believe. The epithets "saint" and "martyr" are given him by the people, properly thinks Lázaro's sister—the narrator of the story and the only other person cognizant of the priest's ideas—since Manuel Bueno has sacrificed his truth to the needs of his people and martyred himself to an ideal in which he did not believe, an ideal—Manuel Bueno would say—which did not exist. "Don Quijote fought for Dulcinea who did not exist."

San Manuel is the last quixotic hero in Unamuno's pages and the most faithful to the Knight of the Mancha. Undeceived and unwilling to deceive himself, he serves an imaginary truth. Yet Angela, the narrator, with a voice more Unamuno's than don Quijote's, objects to the absolute certainty of doubt. For, she writes, "I believe that don Manuel Bueno, my Saint Manuel, and my brother Lázaro died believing that they did not believe that which is most important to us, but without believing they believed, believing with an active and resigned desolation."[32] This apparently contradictory faith pervades the novel but without resolving any doubts. "It is enough for me," don Quijote tells Sancho, "to think and believe that Aldonza Lorenzo is beautiful and good." One does not silence doubts in this way, but one does come to live with an "active and resigned desolation." Manuel Bueno, like Unamuno himself, resigns himself to anguish. But, together with Augusto Pérez of *Niebla* they do not resign themselves to death. Having made his protagonist deny everything, Unamuno salvages the tragic sense of life in Angela's final uncertainty. And the words with which *The Tragic Sense* concludes are addressed as surely to his protagonists and to himself as to his reader: "May God give you, not peace, but glory!"[33]

Courageous, involved in political controversy, the intellectual mentor of a generation in Spain and of legions elsewhere who believe with him that life is the only issue, Unamuno remains a master of paradox. In an age of doubt Unamuno represents for Spaniard and Hispanist alike both a spokesman and a prototype, a Prometheus for modern man.

Another creator of antirational protagonists, Ramón María del Valle-Inclán is also classed by some with the Generation; by others he is viewed as a member of the *modernista* movement; and he is judged by still others to be a unique phenomenon. I belong to the last of these critical schools.

Modernismo, primarily a Latin American movement, revitalized Hispanic poetry by introducing elements from the French parnassian and symbolist traditions, by rediscovering Spanish baroque poetry, and by generally exploring and exploiting the multiple linguistic and imagistic possibilities of language left untouched by the immediately preceding generations. The modernist influence is detectable in all early twentieth-century Spanish poetry, and in his early prose and verse Valle-Inclán is decidedly a *modernista* disciple. But he is considerably more. Recognizing don Ramón's temporal vision of Spain, his satiric genius and his transcendence of the more superficial aspects of *modernismo,* many critics have endeavored to identify him with the Generation.

His mature and truly original works, however, including the original short dramatic form called the *esperpento*, are frantically satiric portraits of contemporary Spain in a style more suggestive of a Victorian Rabelais than of, say, Ganivet's *Conquista.* Valle-Inclán's alter ego, the Marqués de Bradomín, is an early creation. Aptly described as an antihero, he characterizes himself as ugly, sentimental and Catholic. In *Tirano Banderas,* don Ramón created a hero resembling Baroja's protagonists, a man whose forte is adventure and who lives out the dreams of his creator. But the rapport with the Generation ends here, for don Ramón literary skills, as significant as those of his contemporaries, are basically of a different kind.

Don Ramón's nostalgia is not based so much on temporality —as it is for Machado and Azorín—as on mood, atmosphere, or a spiritual state. Laín Entralgo has captured this when he refers to "the presence of or nostalgia for a Galicia half-real and half-dreamed."[34] The emphasis belongs on the second part of the description: Valle-Inclán is concerned not with the frontier of temporal conditions but with the boundary, if any, between reality and fantasy. And Galicia, his native land, the misty and Celtic province of superstition and lore, is one of fantasy's native lands.

While Machado and Azorín struggle with time experienced and time recalled in a Proustian quest for time recaptured, Valle-Inclán uses Galicia and his recollections as a touchstone not for the past but for magic, the possibility of a miraculous world coexisting with the visible world. He evokes Galicia in "El pasajero": "Before the dull Castilian landscape opens the green mystery of a crystalline world."[35] The crystalline world of the four *Sonatas*[36] and *Jardín umbrío* is one aspect of Valle-Inclán's vision. The other is the grotesque mask of Madrid, where folly is mocked, without Ganivet's or Unamuno's philosophic perspective, and chaos is conceived as farce.

Bradomín himself, less an irrational hero than a dandy, is admired and laughed at simultaneously. The figures of the *esperpentos,* with their ridiculous nicknames and their broad gestures, their sinister motives and their gross habits, recall Goya's prints and etchings. Born in society, the object of the author's scorn, they move into another world, a reality of mood and fantasy which is also the world of the *Sonatas.*

The duality of the world known and the world imagined creates a poetic mirage in the *Sonatas;* in the *esperpentos,* a comic apocalypse. There is little resembling the *esperpentos* in the Generation's artistic productions. Only occasioally does the Generation show an interest in radical forms comparable to don Ramón's: Machado in the mock philosophy of Juan de Mairena, Ganivet in his experimental play, Unamuno in *Niebla,* and Azorín in the verbal and structural experimentation of his antinovels.

No less than Goya, Valle-Inclán moves on the margin of many artistic schools with which he holds this or that in common, from which he has learned, and which he has in turn enriched, but he belongs to none. With Goya his merit often lies in making us believe in his magic, leaving us sometimes bewitched and sometimes startled.

No less magical but ideologically one with the Generation, Azorín as essayist and novelist evokes rather than describes his world and his ideas, and this oblique method is not simply a stylistic device: style is not a mere facet of art for Azorín but its essence. This oblique evocation belongs as much to ideology as to description for with Azorín expression is a whole: the idea one with the image articulating it. Both evocation and the identification of idea and image similarly characterize the various periods of his long literary career. *La voluntad (Will),* Azorín's first novel, was published in 1902; major novels appeared throughout the 1940's; his last brief pieces continued almost to his death in 1967. Leon Livingston has established the most effective division of Azorín's novels into three periods: 1) evocation of past reality, 2) evasion of reality and 3) the creation of a subjective, transcendent reality.[37]

Identified with the last of these periods, the novel *El escritor (The Writer)* includes a kind of ars poetica, enumerating the components of Azorín's vision through Antonio Quiroga and

Luis Dávila, the autobiographical protagonists. On one hand Quiroga asserts that "the poet must be above time and space,"[38] but *El escritor* ends with Dávila, the other side of the writer's personality, dedicating himself to an active life of charitable deeds. The novel thus simultaneous documents the author's effort to reconcile life and art as well as his assertion that they are incompatible.

Part of the struggle to fuse experience and creation is the identification of idea and image, and, though Azorín adapts his style to his changing theories, this element remains the same. Azorín creates novels and essays as a painter creates his canvas out of shapes and color. He paraphrases Goethe: "Things are man's frontier."[39] The division between what is self-moving—man—and what is the tool of his will is made by establishing the things which populate the world. In Azorín's hands, this distinction is explored in descriptions whose spiritual dimension is first presented through tangible objects.

These objects acquire dimension through color, the artistic element which most intimately links Azorín to the plastic arts. Since ideas and image are identical, the third dimension, spirit, is created by color. In an early novel, *Las confesiones de un pequeño filósofo (The Confessions of a Little Philosopher)*, the evocation of the past is grounded in a physical evocation of the protagonist, who stands out from the background—from the things which comprise his world—in terms of shapes and colors:

> Reader: I am a little philosopher, I have a silver snuff box full of fine aromatic tobacco, a broad-brimmed hat and a red silk umbrella with a strong steel frame . . . I wish to evoke my life.[40]

The same technique is put to use at the beginning and conclusion of *El caballero inactual (The Uncontemporary Gentleman)*,[41] one of the novels of the last period. A letter from Madrid occasions the action of this actionless novel. As the letter preoccupies the protagonist it increases in size until the white envelope has seized all the rooms of the small summer house. Its whiteness has enveloped the mind as well as the novel.

Concluding the novel, Azorín projects against the blue sky a small white sign—announcing the house is for rent—in such a way as to signify that reality, the limitless horizon, is somehow also for rent. And this movement from the ordinary to the symbolic is a movement of color, a spreading whiteness which fills the canvas, directs the attention, and registers the novel's meaning in a single visual contrast. But it is not only as an evocation of personal moods that Azorín draws meaning out of visual images. Throughout his career the observed world has also been his point of departure for theories of Spain, states of mind, and a cyclic vision of reality.

Azorín's preoccupation with Spain is constant. *Pueblo*, a late novel, definitively evokes his world of "Those who work and suffer." In *Las confesiones*, out of descriptions of the dry, grey, barren, somber town of Yecla emerges an interpretation of the nation:

> And this sadness, century after century, in a poor town . . . has left, in the manner of a millenial sediment, a pervasive sense of sorrow, of mute and passive resignation before the vital struggles of life.[42]

Essays, such as the Inquisitorial scene in *Hora de España* and the descriptions of *Castilla*, continue this identification of national character and national landscape.

Individual as well as national personality is represented in the same way. In *El caballero inactual*, the juxtaposition of objects and colors develops an impression of autumn which in turn introduces four noncharacters, each in terms of a color:

> Autumnus: autumn. The evocative power of that word; weariness, day-dreaming. Autumnus; the year in decline; the land spent, ex-

hausted. Villa-Autumnal: a broad strong stone square. Grey stone and red marble. And two great green circumferences—shadowing pines—about the door, one on each side. Almond trees, straight, swollen with shadow. Within, the parlor's redish light; a clear red, an intense red; a square mass—a table—various square chairs; straight lines; lines that converge and disperse. Haze of red: in the wall, in the carpet. To one side, through the window, blue. Silence, everything brillant, clean. In a lacquered square: crystal, porcelain, silver. The glow of the crystal, of the porcelain and of the silver at play with the angles of light and the red splendor.[43]

But Villa-Autumnal is less a place than a state of mind: the product of the word "autumn," the heaviness of red, the glow of glass and silver, squares, masses of color, and lines of light. For the mature Azorín the structural elements of the known world have become the building blocks of an artistic reality.

Finally the shape and color of the world is the visible demonstration of Nietzsche's myth of the eternal return, adapted to a vision of life compatible with Azorín's more modest philosophy. In "Las nubes" (The Clouds), he uses the repetitious patterns of the sky to anticipate the life patterns which the story describes. In "La ruta de don Quijote" (Don Quijote's Route) he uses the symmetry of the Mancha, the endless repetition of barren landscape and whitewashed towns, to ask the question central to his philosophy: "What is life but a monotonous, inexorable repetition of the same things under different appearances?"[44]

All the elements of Azorín's art are directed toward this question. It is the sense of life repeating itself in fact and transcending itself in art which he seeks to communicate. "I have desired," he affirms, "to write a novel without time, without space and without characters."

Even in his earliest novels and essays, he has evaded traditional forms, so that critics argue whether he has written novels as essays or essays as novels. Ultimately he does write timeless, spaceless, characterless novels. *El caballero inactual* explicitly denies the reality of time and space and intrinsically negates these concepts throughout the novel. Felix Vargas, the novelist-protagonist, inhabits both the contemporary world of Andrea and the sixteenth-century world of the mystic Teresa of Avila. Moreover, he envisions Santa Teresa in the twentieth-century Puerta del Sol of Madrid and willfully confuses Andrea and the saint.

Without regard to sequence, plot or progress, *El caballero inactual* moves from Errondo-Aundi to Villa-Autumnal to Madrid to Biarritz to Avila, not from place to place but from mood to mood. The people too are not distinct characters but moods, facets of the mind, and states of experience. Azorín calls the novel an *etopeya,* a word of his invention related to the Spanish noun for epic, *epopeya,* and best described as a surrealistic epic. This fictional form carries the reader beyond conventional novelistic techniques and the author to the end of his search. As Leon Livingston recognizes, Azorín employs the novel as a personal search, the projection of his consciousness, "the consciousness of the artist, first in search of himself and then in search of the novelist."[45]

The early novels, emphasizing recollection, endeavor to assemble the details of the past in a Proustian fashion. But the novelist continually rejects the significance of self for the significance of art, an art explained in *El escultor* and realized in such novels as *El cabellero inactual* and *La isla sin aurora* (*The Isle without Dawn*). Azorín's search reveals basic patterns of thought for the Generation: will, a sense of time and of death, and a preoccupation with reality.

The struggle between will and the weakness of the will first appears in *La voluntad* with the creation of Antonio Azorín, a character whose personality so dominates that of the author that José Martínez Ruiz began to be known as Azorín. The author did not choose his pseudonym; rather he disappeared into the identity of his fictional creation. The quest described in *El escritor*—"to create a character and make a furious effort to resemble him"—is already partially fulfilled by the absorption of Martínez Ruiz into Azorín. In the end this aim is completely achieved: reality comes to exist only as art and all protagonists, whatever their various names, become the artist, who is again Azorín. Their identification closes another cycle.

But creative will, the challenge of an Unamuno or the irony of a Ganivet, is not to be found in Azorín's pages. Personally and as Spaniard caught up in the sense of time passing—the recognition "that it is always late"—he fatalistically confronts death in his first novel:

> To observe is to feel yourself live and to feel yourself live is to recognize death, to feel the inexorable passage of our entire being and of the things which surround us to the mysterious ocean of Nothingness.[46]

Faced with this sense of the inexorable—Azorín's favorite word—the artist first seeks to find out what reality is and then, having decided that it is art, to preserve it. In both *El escritor* and *El caballero inactual,* the writer-hero asks which is real: the object observed or the object imagined? And each time the latter is chosen.

Imagination is timeless; it gives a perennial dimension to joy as well as to grief; for the contemplative spirit it makes the imagining of things the act of immortalizing them. This is a first step in getting beyond the despair predicated in *La voluntad.*

> To accept the thought of happiness as transitory (as Antonio Azorín has done in *La voluntad*) is to be filled with despair. To stand off and view the pictures of life and self in retrospect was a joyful experience and the true delight of contemplation.[47]

Fiction traditionally imposes a structure which alters even as it immortalizes experience. But Azorín envisions reality as process, the incompleteness of the eternal return, the endless cycle which art may mirror without imposing on it an alien order. This he realizes in an inconclusive novel form: "a purposeful, voluntary containment that corresponds to the imperfection and imperfectability of reality."[48]

The eternity of art is, in Azorín's hands, a fragile eternity, the ephemeral word thrown up against the inexorability of time. In a synoptic passage Valbuena Prat characterizes the world of Azorín as one in which "we die, little by little, and the stones of the Castilian towns and cities grow yellow with age; the memory of a long lost love becomes a resigned grief, and the classic words of literature and the fine thread of language itself fuse to drive a knife of sorrow in our hearts for the sadness of the past."[49]

This is the real world, but for Azorín there is another reality, don Quijote's reality, made of incomparable prose and desperation. It affords a choice, for the world, as Leon Livingston observes, cannot be both real and unreal, but must be potentially both.[50]

The option of art is, perhaps, as valid as the option of experience with its inevitable decay.

Imagination soars through inconcrete space. In a space which we cannot imagine, the design of an inexplicable plan. . . . Where shall we locate that space? . . . Outside of *time, which does not exist,* which is nothing but our sensation. And this sensation, like that of space, is an element in the creative design. Of the supreme, creative will. Creator of a subtle web, complicated, mysterious, made of the sensations which form *that reality in which we live. And that reality does not exist.*[51]

In a world composed of endless cycles and open patterns, of unfulfilled potentials and paradoxes which require no reconciliation as art, man can escape time. In that world, which Machado also perceives but cannot accept, form is truth. And since form is timeless, there, perhaps, it is no longer always late. Such a world would be one of limitless potential, the proper sphere for a man of action. In his dreams Azorín was always such a man; but in fact he was always a man of dreams.

Radically different in style and literary production, Pío Baroja resembles Azorín in this: he too speaks and dreams of men who perform great deeds, but he is not such a man himself. In Baroja the role of artist fuses with that of philosopher but in a manner distinct from Azorín. For Baroja's artist is not above time and space but anchored in the concrete, known world, obliged as creator to struggle with its problems—to muddy his hands in the strife and the labor of his age, as the poet Blas de Otero states his own commitment. In Baroja's hands detail does not define the frontiers of man but rather documents the existential situation in which ideas encounter one another and clash. A descriptive author evoking and propagandizing in his early novels, Baroja progressively becomes a social commentator in the trilogy *La lucha por la vida (The Struggle for Life)*; a social theorist in *Paradox, rey* (*Paradox, the King*); and an existential philosopher in *El árbol de la ciencia* (*The Tree of Knowledge*).[52]

Baroja, like his heroes, has three theories of learning—travel and see, read and see, wander and see—and these three form a single experience. Ideas and observations interact in Baroja's novels until, in his most autobiographical work, *El árbol*, total equilibrium is maintained between Madrid, with its neighboring provincial towns as seen at the end of the nineteenth century, and a Schopenhauerian vision of life.

If Azorín wished to dispense with time, space and characters, Baroja has moved in a different direction, employing each to focus the others. Few novels of ideas—for *El árbol* is at once art and polemic—have maintained so sustained a story line, envisioned so complex a hero, or evoked so vivid a portrait of places and customs. When Anderson Imbert, in an introductory note to the story "Elizabide, el vagabundo," says "after Cervantes, Galdós; after Galdós, Baroja," he properly assesses the Basque's achievement.[53]

Unlike Unamuno, but like Galdós and Cervantes, Baroja never conceives his novels as mere shapes for personal philosophizing. Unlike Azorín he cannot disembody his narrative in a search for abstraction, although he has written many essays on the concept of such novels. For life is not its own explanation: a man's thoughts give it pattern and coherence. In Baroja's major works, act and intention reflect the relationship of art to the existential form of modern thought.

Many of Baroja's works are arranged either in trilogies or in groups bearing titles indicative of the theme which unites the novels: *La lucha por la vida* which is composed of *La busca* (*The Search*), *Mala hierba* (*Weed*) and *Aurora roja* (*Red Dawn*) or *La vida fantástica* consisting of *Aventuras, inventos y mistificaciones de Silvestre Paradox* (*Adventures, inventions and mystifications or hoaxes of Silvestre Paradox*) and *Paradox, rey*. Having so clearly announced his theme, Baroja feels no obligation to subtlety in sustaining it. In his novel of dialogue, *Paradox, rey*, for example, interpolated chapters juxtapose the author's theories with the uninterrupted conversation of the narrative.

In the most formally successful of Baroja's novels, thematic discussion and action are perfectly harmonized. When there is such an accord between idea and spokesman Baroja manages long conversational exchanges without having to name each speaker, an accomplishment indicative of his skill in characterization. The most memorable of Baroja's protagonists are auto-idealizations, not so much autobiographical heroes as prototypes of the man Baroja would have wished to be. They are men of action: pícaros such as Manuel in *La busca*; heroic adventurers such as Martín Zalacain in *Zalacain el aventurero*; participants in the shaping of history, as in the series *Memorias de un hombre de acción* (*Memories of a Man of Action*); philosophers and precursors of a new vision of life, or doomed but still heroic idealists, like César Moncada in *César o nada* (*Caesar or Nothing*) and Andrés Hurtado in *El árbol.*

Increasingly complex, Baroja's protagonists reflect the growing concern of the author with the complexities of life and thought, complexities which ultimately render action impotent. The ideological distance between the Basque self-made man, Zalacain, and the suicidal Andrés Hurtado is measured in an increasingly pessimistic view of mankind and its fate. In *El árbol,* the world will of Schopenhauer becomes the inexorable law of a hostile nature over which the will of man has no ultimate power. In resisting the inevitable, Andrés, in a manner faithful both to don Quijote and to Unamuno, posits doomed resistance against superior truths as a purpose for life, a resistance in which he cannot wholly believe but which is his only answer in the face of fate. As with Ganivet's heroes, Andrés' suicide is an act of will, an ultimate defiance when no other defiance is possible.

Andrés is a man who would change the world, yet who is caught in the tension between what can be dreamed and what can be done. He is finally defeated as much by his own indecision as by external circumstances. Andrés' experience, like Baroja's, includes an education in medicine, life in Madrid and in the provinces, philosophic study, loneliness and wandering, the frustration of plans to renew society, and final despair.

In the death of Martín Zalacain, the nonreflective man of action, a romantic ideal is laid to rest. The death of Zalacain is tragic because it is in heroic acts that his valor is measured; but the death of Andrés is a beginning and his valor consists in his striking out against a fate recognized but defied. The doctor who pronounces him dead observes: "There was in him something of the precursor."[54]

Even as Andrés' death is, in its way, heroic, it remains immeasurably distant from the symbolic death of Ganivet's Pedro Mártir, since Andrés' protest is a pale reflection of the Nietzschean creed expounded by Ganivet. Twenty-five years later, Andrés is merely an echo of that affirmation, the hollow voice of an alienated and powerless man crying out against a hostile fate, the epitome of Baroja's frustrated heroes.

Ganivet's hero dies to be immortal; Baroja's Andrés dies simply because there is no protest to be made except his own suicide. The thesis—one robs death of its domination by choosing to die—is the same: Ganivet's choice is conceived as triumph, the rebellion of man against the gods; Baroja's protest sounds from the depths, where a conquered figure shakes his fist at an indifferent cosmos.

Even if the stature of man is shrunk to infinitesimal insignificance, man is still a rebel. Baroja has made of the eternal return, the basis of Azorín's creative theory, a cycle of destruction and creation from which the human will—Ganivet's and Unamuno's hope—is irrevocably excluded. Ganivet has said that everything is possible, and so man must dare all things in order to be free. Everything is impossible, Baroja declares, and so man must continue to protest or else cease to be man.

It is in this context, born in affirmation and ending in doomed protest, surrounded by visions of fate, doubt, and search that Antonio Machado wrote, a gentler man than his contemporaries, neither affirming nor despairing, a voice continually asking for answers to an as yet unanswered question. Machado's questions offer a kind of hope, a final possibility in a nihilistic age.

Machado's life at moments touched upon the lives of his contemporaries. Capturing the uniqueness of Valle-Inclán's work and personality, he calls him "Charon / with the eyes of fire, the funereal boatman / of Acheron's churning waters."[55] Unamuno he portrays as a hammer forging a new Spain and a voice summoning his forces on with cries of "Forward."[56] But Azorín he evokes as a lover of ancient Spain, the Spain of tradition, yet also a fellow dreamer of change, of transformation, and of the birth of a new Spaniard.[57]

Born in Seville, Machado spent part of his youth in Giner de los Ríos' Instituto Libre de Enseñanza and another part in Paris, the poetic center of his time. Rubén Darío, the major *modernista* poet, was in Paris at the time reading the compositions of aspiring poets who came seeking his judgment and approval. The modernist influence is partial in Machado's work, whereas in the poetry of his brother Manuel it is pronounced and primary. Although he admired Darío, Machado, as he states in one of his prefaces, envisioned a different course for his own work.[58]

The division of interest between the modernists and Machado is primarily a philosophic one. Pure modernism is an almost wholly aesthetic phenomenon. Machado's concerns are too metaphysical to be satisfied by such an approach, in spite of his obvious and necessary preoccupation with metric and imagistic experiment. Yet Machado is not a professional intellectual as Unamuno was. By profession he was a secondary-school French teacher. In 1911, shortly after his marriage, he studied with Bergson in Paris, having received a grant from the Spanish government for that purpose. His serious association with philosophy dates from this period, although his enthusiasm for Bergson subsequently cooled. Later, he took a doctoral degree in philosophy at the University of Madrid and became the first Spaniard to comment upon the works of Martin Heidegger.

Machado's poetry is extremely personal, intimately involving his concern for Spain, his interest in particular philosophers, and a few personal experiences. He briefly collaborated with his brother on a few plays; in one of these he acknowledges autobiographical details.[59]

But the major events of his life which acquire poetic meaning are his marriage and the death of his wife Leonor in 1912, whose memory thereafter dominated Machado's poetry. This influence is evident from the second edition of *Campos de Castilla*, the first edition of which had appeared shortly before Leonor's death. Later in his career, when teaching in Segovia (after a period in the Andalusian city of Baeza), his publications included poems dedicated to an unidentified love, called in these poems and in subsequently discovered letters, Guiomar, a married friend recently identified as Pilar Valderrama and whose role in Machado's life is still a matter of controversy.[60]

For his prose work, Machado invented a pen name and alter ego, Juan de Mairena, identified as a gymnastics teacher who gave lectures in metaphysics as a sideline. The jesting tone of this description prevails throughout the articles and notes attributed to Mairena, a kind of philosophy of life delivered tongue-in-cheek. Mairena, in turn, speaks of yet another alter ego, whom he identifies as his (Mairena's) teacher, one Abel Martín, author of a seven volume work on ontology, a work yet to be read by anyone in its entirety. The names Juan de Mairena and Abel Martín appear in Machado's poetry and one volume, the *Cancionero apócrifo* (*The Apocryphal Anthology*) was attributed to Martín.[61]

Politically committed from his youth to the concept of a republic in Spain, Machado remained an active supporter of Negrín's government until the end of the Spanish Civil War, writing for the militantly pro-Republican magazine *Hora de España*. When the Republic fell in Barcelona, Machado crossed the Pyrenees, arriving at an internment camp in Collioure, France, on January 28, 1939.[62] On February 22 he died there, joining Unamuno, Valle-Inclán and García Lorca in the lists of the Spanish intellectuals whose lives were claimed directly or indirectly by that conflict. When Hugh Thomas, in his book on the Spanish Civil War, enumerates the casualties of each political party, he concludes that no group suffered more than that of the poets.[63]

Of the Generation of '98, Ganivet had died long before the Second Republic; Unamuno and Machado perished as the struggle of the Republic was waged; Baroja and Azorín lived to see decades of change in Spain. Obviously a time of rapid transition has altered the views of those members of the Generation who survived the Civil War. But the constants which made a cohesive reality of the Generation of '98 are of a kind which neither war nor the passage of time can alter: love of country, search for truth, existential doubt and personal affirmation, personal despair and personal anguish. For the Generation did not write simply for a moment in history. Essentially all of these men wrote from a vital concern for the human condition, transcending their own age in the transcendence of their theme.

Nature as an Expression of Temporality

THE DUSTY white road, rising from the banks of the Duero into the mountains, commands a view of Soria with its old houses and, across the river, of a crumbling castle and the deserted cloister of San Juan del Duero, beneath the massive peaks of Moncayo, Espino and Urbión. Reading Machado's *Campos de Castilla*, one can recreate the scene in many ways: the crisp chill of early March, an April drizzle, the delicate adornment of spring flowers, the penetrating sun of a July afternoon, the gray barrenness of late autumn. And yet, although he remains faithful to the physical appearance of this landscape—as to that of Seville and Baeza—the emotional response to nature itself which the poet communicates is incidental. Essentially Machado articulates a personal vision and portrays the Spanish soul through the visible world. As El Greco's *View of Toledo* is the visualization of Spain's sixteenth-century mystical spirit, Machado's landscapes exteriorize his own memories and hopes, and the Spain of the late nineteenth and early twentieth centuries for which he grieves: "Sad lands / so sad as to have a soul."[1]

This sadness which hovers over all experience, individual and national, is the product of time, life's determinant and, according to Machado's alter ego, Juan de Mairena, ultimate reality.[2] So essential to the poet's vision is his awareness of temporality that he describes poetry as a dialogue of man with time,[3] acknowledging its destructiveness as well as the consolation of memory and hope: "To live is to devour time; to hope."[4] Man thus encounters the paradox of temporal existence: life simultaneously consumes itself and begets hope. "Without time, that invention of Satan . . . the world would lose the anguish of waiting and the consolation of hope. Then the devil would have nothing to do, nor would the poets."[5] Machado implies that if time is ultimate truth, poetry approaches that truth by expressing the multiple relationships between loss and hope, time's offspring. At the same time, each poem is a creative act which gives substance to subjective reality and becomes for man, in Juan de Mairena's words, "a visionary act, the affirmation of an absolute reality."[6]

This subjective reality primarily involves circumstances of the poet's own life, his desires and recollections. Nostalgia for the countryside of his youth prevades his work, even the last sonnets: "My childhood Seville, how Sevillan you were / how time would gnaw your memory but all in vain."[7] The memory of his wife Leonor persists in images of the Sorian countryside. Thus, although Machado left Soria almost immediately after Leonor's death to teach in Baeza and later in Segovia, that landscape is always spiritually present for him: "My heart dwells where it was born / not to life but to love by the Duero's shore."[8]

Spain too is mirrored in the poet's sense of temporality, in those attitudes which describe Machado as a member of the Generation of 1898. His interpretations of the present in terms of history and the character of the Spaniard suggest Ganivet's and Unamuno's theories of history and "intra-history." His disgust with contemporary society, "wounded Spain, dressed up for carnival,"[9] parallels the attitudes of Azorín who described Spain as living in a century of mystification,[10] and of Baroja, who pictured his compatriots as mired in apathy and false optimism. So too, Unamuno's call for the creative, irrational dedication of don Quijote in his countrymen echoes in Machado's challenge: "You, youth . . . will go to your adventure / awake and transparent before the divine light."[11]

For this vision of self and of Spain the poet derives a form from the physical world, tangible and defined. Concerned with life both as being and as transition, he perceives that in some facets of nature existence and movement are identical. In the images of water he sees both the nourishment of the land which nature provides and the endless repetition of the fountain which is, simultaneously, his touchstone for memories of a Sevillan childhood. Water becomes the symbol of nascent life and of love. In a poem to Guiomar the poet speaks of love engendered in gardens above the river. The growth of life, its continuity and its capacity for birth become one with the rivers, fountains and life-giving rain of the harsh Spanish landscape.

Older than the poet's personal recollection is the symbol of life as river and the sea as death. From the late medieval poet Jorge Manrique Machado takes this image and fuses it with his own experience of water as a source of life in the barren land. Never reconciled, the two images persist throughout Machado's work: the irrevocable journey of the river to the sea; the eternal repetition of the ageless fountain.

Roads too are contradictory images. There is Dante's road, symbol of life which must end. But another road exists, vaguely perceived, the final distant image of innumerable poems. In dreams, roads continue, conquering the uncertainty as well as the agony of life. Both in dreams and in conscious experience the road is a symbol of the human search, an existential pursuit which Machado conceives as a philosopher and articulates as a poet in the image of white Castilian paths.

Because the poet knows only past experience with certainty and searches in a vague, insecure world, he travels in the afternoon of life, enveloped in shadow. He sees renewal in the traditional image of dawn but, uniquely, as he perceives the promise of the future in recollections of the past, so too he anticipates the light of the dawn in the light of the setting sun. Anticipating his own hope he asks, "What are you seeking, poet, in the West?"[12]

The constant juxtaposition of end and beginning, the sunset which is the necessary prelude to sunrise, repeats the poet's complex temporal consciousness. It is only because the day ends that the day can begin again; and only because there are cycles in nature can man believe in the cyclic process.

Like dawn, spring is the completion of the cycle, the promise of life beyond death and the only evidence man possesses of a continually renascent reality. As Leonor dies Machado writes that he awaits "*another* miracle of spring." The first is in nature; the other is speculative.

His most effective poems and his major images end in uncertainty. Water is the flow of the river to soundless sea and the source of life; roads signify our mortal existence and also continuity; nature is reborn and man may therefore hope—but never with certainty of fulfillment—also to be reborn.

In doubt and in a dream, the world of suspended objectivity, the poet carries on his dialogue with time, a conversation originating in the familiar landscape and ultimately confronting the unknown. The stages of the dialogue—personal, poetic and metaphysical—are resumed in the sonnet sequence "Los sueños dialogados" (The Dream Dialogues). But they end with a question. The only certainty the poet knows is the tangible world which gives form to the dialogue.

When applied to Spain, images of nature both evoke Castile's physical reality and describe metaphorically Machado's interpretation of history and his ideals for his country. He evokes his contemporaries in images of the landscape and considers with them the contrast between past glory and present decay. A recurring theme in the poems concerning Soria, this emphasis on history finds its most complete expression in "A orillas del Duero" (On the Duero's Banks) where vision, landscape and a theory of history unite.

Bitterness over his nation's plight, its hollow pride and what he deems its characteristic vices is communicated in direct statements, in the allegorical ballad "La tierra de Alvargonzález" and in poems written, as if in fulfillment of a prophecy, during the Civil War.

Both personally and as interpreter of Spain, Machado measures temporal distances and balances temporal contrasts: loss, possession, hope; glory, stagnation, potential. As physical vision can measure spatial distance, poetic vision perceives temporal distance: "All poetry is seeing," writes Machado, "and such vision requires distance."[13] Concepts of and words for space consistently acquire temporal connotations; words such as diminutives, which suggest spatial distance, evoke temporal distinctions; descriptions which reach out over the landscape move from one temporal reality to another. At the same time they suggest the contrasts of destruction and creation. Nature reveals temporal continuity, which is the context of man's sorrow and his expectation.

In the majority of Machado's poems nature is a specific landscape. Even in "Los sueños dialogados" the symbolic language of the sonnets is grounded in the contrast between the harsh countryside of Soria and the fertile land of Baeza. In a few poems, however, the world evoked is almost entirely abstract: a world in dreams, a landscape without identity. This is true, for example, of several poems based upon the road images, as "Sobre la tierra amarga" (Above the Bitter Earth) and in a number of the late poems attributed to Abel Martín.[14]

Also abstract and restating many of Machado's most frequent images is the poem "Y no es verdad, dolor" which can serve both as an example of the intricacy of Machado's total vision and as a résumé of predominant themes and metaphors:

> And it is not true, sorrow, I know
> you well, nostalgia for a life that's lost,
> and solitude of shadowed heart,
> of ship still safe and starless still.
>
> As a lost dog that has not track
> nor scent and wanders
> far on roads, without a road, as
> too the child who on a festive night
>
> is lost amid the crowd,
> the dusty air and candle sparks, and
> overwhelmed is and startled in his
> heart by music and by grief,
>
> thus do I go, melancholy now and drunk,
> guitarist mad and poet too and
> poor man who in dreams
> shall ever seek for God within the mist.[15]

That Machado begins by acknowledging sorrow is no surprise: grief is a theme in his work from the earliest poems. What is surprising is the initial word, not required for the meter since the hendecasyllabic line would scan as easily by employing the anticipated hiatus between "no" and "es."* Obviously the opening conjunction is not gratuitous but rather suggests a continuity with a larger context, the total experience out of which the poem arises and in which both the familiarity with sorrow and the abstractions of the poem can be justified. As one conversant with

1 2 3 4 5 6 7 8 9 10 11 1 2 3
* Y / no es / ver / dad / do / lor / yo / te / co / noz / co or No / es / ver
4 5 6 7 8 9 10 11
/ dad / do / lor / yo / te / co / noz / co.

grief throughout his life, the poet articulates the four quatrains which comprise this poem as part of a longer conversation.

Having established his relationship with sorrow, he seeks to define the nature and thus the source of his sadness. The terms in which he does so are closely linked to time, both explicitly in the word "nostalgia" and implicitly in images which, here as throughout Machado's work, suggest uncertainty (shadowed) and unguided wandering (starless). But time, Machado has said, inspires more than despair; it also inspires hope. And so the uncharted wandering is not disaster ("still safe"; the Spanish says literally "not shipwrecked"); it is merely uncertain.

From this first quatrain the tenor of the poem is established: doubt, vagueness, search, loss, grief. The interplay of the search and the sense of uncertainty in which it is undertaken are developed in the remaining three quatrains, which form a unit. Their cohesiveness is apparent in the enjambment which ties the final phrase of the second stanza to the first words of the third and which concludes the ideas of the second and third stanzas in the clause with which the final stanza opens (*thus* do I go).

But whereas the initial mood is one of familiarity with sorrow and inconclusiveness—both the first and the last words suggest incompleteness—the last stanza stresses continuity in spite of the chaos in which the search for truth must be made. The movement from acknowledged sorrow to quixotic quest is reiterated in the movement represented physically throughout the poem: in the enjambed lines, in the images of wandering ship, lost dog and lost child. Because the rhyme scheme is assonant (in e, a) and a translation need reproduce only the approximate structure and rhythm of the original, it is possible to retain in translation all the poetic devices, most word position and imagery.

In the development of the quatrains, images and word position are significant because the poet extends his theme with each image and further expands his discussion of each, increasing narrative speed and intensifying his total impression. The first image of the ship without a star occupies a single line and contains both aspects of the quest: the ship has neither run aground nor found its way.

The second image, that of the wandering dog, is developed in three lines with repetition of the word *road* (wanders / far on roads, without a road) emphasizing that the dog goes on searching but that he has no path to follow.

Again in the second stanza the poet introduces a synonymous image—that of the lost child—to which the third quatrain is entirely devoted. We receive a complete description, richer in evocation and in symbol than the previous metaphors. Yet the context has not really changed. It is still dark. The starless night, the shadowed heart of the solitary poet are reiterated in the night scene with its artificial lights through which the lost child moves. The context is, of course, more human: the ship and the lost dog are symbols of the questing poet but the child is his personification, frightened as a ship cannot be and as a dog may be only in a less complex manner.

The child, therefore, brings us back to the initial human recognition of sorrow. The last line evokes both the artistic world (music) and the thematic grief. In progressing from the initial avowal to his conclusion, the poet has not merely repeated himself. Rather he has resumed the images which comprise his treatment of the human search: the ship upon the sea, the uncharted road, the vagueness of night, shadows and nostalgia.

In this world of evocation and wandering the poet can conclude by listing anew the elements of his poem. As he gives himself identities in the last stanza he also repeats the principal images of the poem. The first and final stanzas emphasize that, in spite of the metaphors, the poem is personal, now an affirmation of grief, now of quest: *I* know you; thus do *I* go.

The description *drunk* also relates to the lack of a clear sense of direction, present in the first stanza in the image *starless,* for this lack of guidance leaves the ship as lost as the drunkard, and also to the dog who has lost the sense of smell which ought to guide it. The word *melancholy* immediately recalls the nostalgia mentioned in the first stanza. The mad guitarist recalls the child startled by music and by grief as well as the unwrecked ship moving aimlessly through the darkness. No one of the three images is in a position to employ logic or rationality to extract itself from the enveloping uncertainty.

The embodiment of such a lost soul, without recourse to logic, is the poet, and when he is mentioned the series of identifications is almost concluded. There is one more name for the poet, a name that reaffirms the irrational character of all the poem's images and of the quest itself. That is the dream image (poor man in dreams). For the poet can seek God—Machado's symbol for truth—only within his poetic function, only as vision, never as rational conclusion nor as deduction nor as something meaningful outside the dream.

The quest is, then, a definitively human one, subjective in all its aspects, in its nature, in its representation, and in its goal. For Machado does not say that he seeks truth as an idea. In a singularly nonreligious poem by a nonreligious poet, truth is named God, for a god is a personal truth, the subjective name for the goal of a subjective quest, undertaken in the irrational world called by the poet a dream.

Balanced by the use of the first person singular in the opening and concluding stanzas, by the repetition of images, by the development of a sense of loss and search, and by movement from sorrow recognized to the quest undertaken (not so much in spite of as in cognizance of sorrow), the poem is also balanced by the employment of a Renaissance verse form based on the hendecasyllable and its hemistich, in this case 7 syllable. The hemistich moves up, as it were, in the stanza, becoming the brief introductory line for the long thematic conclusion of the first stanza. In the second stanza the hemistich contributes—as second line—principally to the sense of movement by underscoring the embambment. In the third, where continuity of images is still the rule, the hemistich, moving as the poem moves, has progressed to the first position in the quatrain, where it serves as a bridge between the end of the second stanza and the subject of the third, which is a development of the preceding line. In the last stanza, however, the hemistich is back in the original position, serving as third line both to suggest a parallel between initial and final concepts of the poem and to stress, as in the first quatrain, the significance of the last line.

The third lines in the opening and closing stanzas are complimentary not merely in function but also in meaning. Since Machado repeatedly uses shadow images to suggest dreams, the "solitude of shadowed heart" anticipates the later image of "poor man in dreams." The last lines in these two stanzas are also similarly related. The "ship still safe and starless still" suggests in the final line an incompleteness made purposeful as quest.

In this poem metrical and structural development, therefore, signify, as completely as the imagery, the poem's total vision, united at the outset to the poet's experiences by the evocative conjunction *and* and joined to his continuing experience at the conclusion by the image of eternal search in an uncertainty (mist) no more hopeful than the starless image of the beginning but—Machado would be quick to add—no more hopeless.

This tension between vague hope and implicit hopelessness characterizes many of Machado's personal as well as national poems. But it would be unfair to the poet tacitly to suggest that the mood of anguish and skepticism, evident in the majority of the time-oriented poems, is completely descriptive of his work. Humor, for example, present above all in the prose attributed to

Juan de Mairena, is not simply a second and distinct facet of the poet. Rather Machado grasps simultaneously the agony and the irony of life. His humor, like Chekov's, springs from the pathetic in reality with its comic and tragic overtones.

Man in time is an eminently pathetic figure: nothing in life or in the world around him possesses absolute permanence. The poet's preoccupation with this impermanence and with the uncertainty of human understanding unify his theme, expressed through the temporal conditions of nature. We do not suggest that any of Machado's images is static or invariably used in the same manner to express the same thing. Nevertheless, since the conditions described are themselves defined, the images employed will of necessity be fairly consistent.

We will be concerned with these images and their temporal implications in the chapters which follow, especially images of water, of roads, cycles of the day and of the year, and the sonnet sequence on the dream dialoque as well as poems which apply these images to Spain and national problems, bearing in mind that Machado begs of the critic "an ardent desire to see realized a miracle of beauty."[16] For every critical venture is at once a cooperative and a creative one, or as Northrop Frye phrases it, "allegorical interpretation, an attaching of ideas to the structure of poetic imagery."[17]

Images and Cycles

SINCE the temporality of life is central to Machado's thought, his poetic expression of every aspect of life reflects this idea. Thus, for him, everything in nature primarily reflects change. It is the familiar, ever varying countryside through which he was accustomed to walk, hour upon hour, which becomes, almost inevitably, the substantial form of his poetic vision: its life process, a projection of his own; and its images, an extended pathetic fallacy.

In this association of the physical and spiritual worlds, images of water are used to express the temporal conditions of human life: genesis, being and becoming. Rain and all water which, as it flows through the land, nourishes trees and plants, possess the same creative power which man recognizes in his grief, in his hope, and in his love. Fountains of stone and marble, associated with scenes of the poet's youth, suggest the relationship of the past to the present, and the water which continually pours from them, a sense of continuity. In reflecting both upon genesis and upon past experience, Machado is conscious that subjective interpretation limits and deforms his understanding. Indeed, each moment alters this interpretation because life is in constant movement. This journey, from unknown origin to unknown end, takes the conventional form of a river destined for the sea.

Lacking Manrique's religious convictions, Machado can agree only that: "Our lives are rivers / which flow to the sea / that is death," but not that beyond death there awaits certain immortality.

Unamuno has described three possible human reactions to death:

> a) either I know that I die completely and with that knowledge, irremediable despair, b) or I know that death is not absolute and thus I am resigned to it, or c) I cannot know either with certainty and thus I experience resignation in despair or vice versa: a despairing resignation or a resigned despair and its resultant struggle.[1]

Machado belongs in the last of these states, although his own inquiry into the nature of dying is not so much a struggle as a desire for self-realization, transcending the limitations of time. This desire and the coexistent awareness of death lie at the core of Machado's poetry.

This does not mean that life is purely tragic, since essential to any sense of time is an awareness of things coming to be. Change is beneficent when, like rain or water flowing through the fields, it generates life. Living among the Sorian peasants, for whom a generous rainfall means the difference between a year of absolute misery and a plentiful harvest, Machado asks of a winter rain "Oh, good water, leave life / in your passing"[2] and senses youthful vigor and joy in a spring shower:

April contains a thousand rains.
A threatening wind sweeps the sky
and between this cloud and that on high
splashes blue as indigo stains.

Water and sky. The rainbow bright.
Against a distant cloud
zig-zaps
a clear yellow light.

The rain upon the window loud-
ly plays and nags.

O'er and through the haze
spun all of rainy sprays
meadows green from mist arise,
appears an oak grove from the maze,
a mountain grey into mist dies.

The rain shower's fibrous spray
slants down upon the frond bed
and whips the stagnant water shed
where the Duero its torrent lay.

On fertile earth the raindrops smite
as on the craggy new-sown fields,
over the oaks the clouds may yield
and sun the highway puddles light.

Rain and sun. Now the field
grows dark and now grows bright,
here a mountain fades from sight,
quickly there a hill's revealed.

Now illumined, now made grey,
scattered ranches dot the way,
distant towers spring to view.

Toward the leaden mountains play-
ful rush, each other to pursue,
clouds of cotton-white and ashen-grey.[3]

Everything in nature seems to be playful, or, to borrow Machado's phrase, "rather than young, adolescent."[4] The constant changing of rhyme pattern, the interplay of descriptive line and staccato observations (Water and sky. The rainbow bright.)

with the accompanying changes of stress, make the form as elusive as the landscape that disappears and reappears ("appears an oak grove from the maze, / a mountain grey into mist dies") with the sudden shifts of sun and shadow, and the erratic gaiety of a lightning flash ("Against a distant cloud / zig-zaps / a clear yellow light."), or the sky which appears momentarily amid the clouds. Neither the landscape nor the lines themselves behave in a disciplined manner; the internal rhyme in the opening line introduces a mood of spontaneity in which neither length of line nor length of stanza is bound to any absolute norm. Each stanza is a vignette, an elaboration of the abundance and variety implicit in the image of "a thousand rains." Nor is the final stanza a conclusion, since the vitality of nature is still abroad in the clouds which continue rolling toward the mountains.

Rain, gray clouds and indigo blue skies connote gaiety and joy because they bring vitality and abundance to the land. This life-giving property of rain is related directly to (or by comparison with) a human situation:

> Good tears once spilled
> for a youthful love
> as the April fields are washed
> by fresh clouds above.
>
> . . . . .
>
> tears that joyous rise
> as in the fountain cries
> the sonorous water's voice.[5]

The stanza not only equates tears with rain, but also identifies the tears with the effects of April rain on the fields. Just as the rain revitalizes the land and promotes new life, so those youthful tears were also creative of new hopes. Such sorrow was innocence: the tears shed rose purified as new joys. In that yesterday every experience was a living source; today, innocence lost in some little wisdom, the poet has also lost the promise which youth held:

> Yesterday poet, today poor and sad,
> defunct philosopher, he who has sold
> for coins made of copper all that he had,
> exchanged in ill bargain, yesterday's gold.[6]

But the promise of joy in life, like the promise of nature's bounty in water, is not limited to youth. Love too is a genesis:

> The valley roads to river go
> and there, by the stream, love has been.
> Does the field its youthful garments show
> for you, companion never seen?
>
> . . . . .
>
> it is you who blossom and awake.[7]

The brief prose commentary, attributed to Machado's alter ego, Abel Martín, advances a theory of love: "The beloved is . . . in a sense, one with the lover, not at the end . . . of the erotic process but in its beginning,"[8] which the poet communicates as an experience. The transformation of nature is physically dependent upon the nourishment of the river; but the human emotion too is described as part of nature. Spring and love are born of the same source because the lover seeks a tangible realization of his desire, and spring is the desired made visible. Thus is the beloved ("companion never seen") identical with the poet as the object of a desire incarnate in nature. And just as the river is the source both of love and of spring, the beloved is responsible for the vitality of nature and the eroticism of the poet. But even as spring has its origin in the object of the poet's emotion, his love attains fulfillment in the physical reality of nature. For, to Abel Martín, love and the physical world are inseparable:

You, lovers, woven are of spring
of earth and water, wind and sun are spun.
The mountains in your breathless bosoms sing
and in your eyes, flower fields beneath the sun.[9]

As love waits "by the stream," drawing life from that water which sustains nature, so the lovers also appear as products ("woven") of spring's formative elements: the soil, water, wind and sun, which generate the fullness of nature's life. Similarly, as elements of man's fundamental nature, emotions create love, which is the essence of human life. In the spiritual landscape, which here corresponds to and becomes identical with the visible landscape, just as nature transforms itself, the lovers are transformed by the emotion born in them. The external and internal worlds appear to fuse so that nature is reflected in man and the lovers participate in the beauty that is spring.

This genesis of love does not appear as a theme in Machado's early poetry, nor does it refer to his wife Leonor. The songs of a personal eroticism, whose object the poet identified only as Guiomar, are heard in the last decade of his life.[10] Both reality and dream, this love is also manifested in a world which is itself created by the lover's dream:

In a garden have I dreamed of you,
high above the river, Guiomar,
the garden of a time-enclosèd view
with gates of iron for its bar.

An unfamiliar bird is heard
sweetly in the nettletree to sing
beside the water's good and living word
all thirst and all fountains there to bring.

There, Guiomar, in the garden place,
our mutual garden, jointly made
two hearts attuned embrace
and fused are and interlaid
the hours of our day . . .[11]

Again this is a landscape with all the properties necessary for life, but it is born of the encounter of two people in love, for whom the whole world is subject to their emotion and to their invention. Both the physical context—the garden—and the human—time—are enclosed ("the garden of a time-enclosėd view / with gates of iron for its bar") by the complexion of love. Inasmuch as love is aware only of its object, the garden in which it thrives is separated from the rest of the world. And since the erotic fusing of two individual lives ("and fused are and interlaid / the hours of our day") creates a new reality ("our mutual garden, jointly made"), which contains its own desire and its own fulfillment ("all thirst and all fountains"), that reality is sheltered from the temporality which haunts life.

This shelter does not, however, erase the images of time: memory of days forever lost, awareness of man's imperfect understanding of the past and his fragile hopes for the future, and a sense of life's precipitous journey to its end. If all aspects of man's milieu grew old homogeneously, this change could take place almost imperceptively. It is the contrast between the changing and the constant which accentuates our sense of time, yet, at the same time, intensifies our memory. For Machado the images which were familiar parts of his youth and which have remained relatively unchanged through the years are points of contact with that youth. Thus, a marble fountain linking experience of the past with the present permits the poet to converse with this enduring past:

. . . . The fountain water's flight
monotonously over the marble white.
The fountain sang: Brother, do you know
a distant dream in my present song?
It was a slow afternoon of summer slow.

. . . . .

It was this day; and water leapt in me
as now on cold marble the same monotony.

. . . . .

(poet:) Tell me forgotten legends, full of joy.
—I know not legend of some former bliss
but of melancholy, old tales that tell of this.

Your lips, burning, your grief affirm,
today's thirst was yesterday's thirst in turn.[12]

But the past has no tale of joy to tell, such as the poet seeks. It preserves only sorrows and unfulfilled desires, made doubly bitter by the awareness that these desires remain unfulfilled: "today's thirst was yesterday's thirst in turn."

In all grief, Machado declares, there is a continuity like the interminable jet of water that rises from the stone fountain:

I listen to the song
of ancient cadence made
which children sing.

. . . . .

The songs confuse
the tale but yet retain
the grief within
as, clear, the water
bears its tale
of love now old,
that never singer told.

. . . . .

The fountain made of stone
forth sends its endless
flow of love and tales.

. . . . .

The story onward goes;
the fountain's still,
the tale's erased
but grief still speaks.[13]

Both the songs which the children sing and the fountain belong to a distant past reaching into the present, but in each case a part of reality has been lost. The past, symbolized by the fountains, has witnessed many experiences whose particulars have been obscured and lost with the passage of time, like the stories in the children's songs ("The songs confuse / the tale but yet retain / the grief within"). And just as the sense of grief endures in these tales, so that which becomes eternal in the fountain is also sorrow. What is true of the folktales can be said of all life, since the description first applied to these songs ("the songs confuse / the tale . . ."), through the comparison of the emotion and the physical quality of the water ("but yet retain / the grief within / as, clear, the water / bears its tale / of love . . ."), is completed in the last stanza with the tale which the fountain repeats of all human experience: only sorrow endures.

Melancholy, like the voices of a fountain, is older than particular tales of sadness; older, too, than the songs which celebrate these tales; and when the tale and the song are silent, the emotion, like the fountain, remains:

It was a night in May,
blue the sky and serene,
above the lean cypress' sway,
a full moon's light was seen,

and fountain stone its light to rob
where in the waters rise and fall
in lonely intermittent sob.
Sounds now only the fountain's call.

And dulcet there a melody
wanders through the garden all:

It was lament harmonious;
of youth it sang and love.

"The garden has a fountain cold,
a chimera to it belongs.
Spring's soul, its tale is told
as sad voice chants its songs."

Ceased the voice and silent fell
the violin's lovely strain.
Yet melancholy did remain
wandering through the garden's dell.
Nought is heard but fount's refrain.[14]

The voice of the fountain encompasses the entire poem; it is present not only before, together with and after the melodies of singer and violin, but also in the lover's tale of youth and love ("The garden has a fountain cold . . ."). In it, grief is heard before the first notes of the lament sound. Both the violin's melody and the sad voice, as well as the youthful love they celebrate, belong to the moment, but the melancholy in which they have participated, like the fountain, transcends the momentary ("Yet melancholy did remain . . ."). Again, only sadness endures.

This sadness is inherent in the transiency of all things, since memory does not restore the past nor represent it objectively, but rather presents a series of ever-changing subjective interpretations. Seek the joys you know; you shall find they are gone. Recall your youthful aspirations; you shall perceive that realizations were few and momentary. Man passes through life always pursuing the same desires. Thus he is always essentially alone, like one who stands amidst shadows in a silence broken only by the monotony of a gushing fountain:

> In the middle of the plaza and on rough stone
> the water ceaseless spouts. In the garden nest
> beneath the wine-entangled wall, a lone
> tall cypress raises its stiff foliage crest.
>
> The afternoon sets where the great houses stand
> in the wide plaza wrapt in dream. There gleam
> on windowpanes the dying echoes of the sun. And
> on the balcony, forms vague as death's heads beam.
>
> The calm is infinite in that deserted place
> where the soul its image draws of soul in pain,
> the water spouts repeatedly within its marble vase.
> In all the air, no sound save the water breaks again.[15]

Here solitude and stillness are emphasized by the rigid image of a single cypress, the grotesque shadows discerned on balconies surrounding the empty plaza, and the lone voice of the fountain. As Carlos Bousoño points out, discussing Machado in his *Teoría de la expresión poética*: "Solitude is best expressed by means of contrast, through the contemplation of a single object rather than a thoroughly deserted scene."[16] These images, moreover, contribute not only to the solitude of the scene but also to its sense of anguish: they define the somber background for human experience ("where the soul its image draws of soul in pain"). Just as the plaza is enclosed by buildings, implied in the references to balconies and the ivy-covered wall, the solitary poet is walled in by time. Life flees in the growing obscurity of the scene ("the afternoon sets . . ." / "dying echoes of the sun"), in the brevity and finality of the images, but above all in the acute contrast between the dying afternoon and the unaltered rhythm of the water in the marble fountain.

Life is constantly in flight, from an unknown origin to an unknown end: "To know, we nothing know / we come from a remote sea, / and to an unknown sea we go."[17] The poet is able to reflect upon this journey and thus upon the essence of his life, but without a clear vision of that essence:

Where the poor river ends the immense sea awaits.

. . . . .

Beneath the bridge's bay the shadowed water passes by.
(It is my soul, thought I!)
And so I halted there a moment, alone,
in the afternoon, in reverie . . .
What is this drop, in the wild wind blown,
that cries out to the sea: am I the sea?[18]

Everything which is said here of the river becomes meaningful in terms of a spiritual reality by identifying the water as one's soul. First, just as he observes the water's movement with respect to a fixed object, the bridge beneath which it passes, so from the vantage point of a particular moment in his life the poet is aware of and able to contemplate the meaning of life in flux. But the shadow of self in the present, like the shadow of the bridge, falls across the vision, so that what he sees and understands is only "shadowed water." Thus the little wisdom which life itself possesses is tragic: we are all part of a pitiful journey in which we are certain only that the journey will end. Whoever seeks to know himself cries out against the hostile and alien world to the unknown ("this drop, in the wild wind blown / that cries out to the sea"). For the resistence to extinction and the desire for understanding are an intimate part of the human situation:

Every man has two
battles to wage.
In dreams with God contends
and waking struggles with the sea.[19]

Caught between blind confidence, untenable to the skeptic, and utter despair, Machado approaches here more than in any other poem Unamuno's position: "I cannot know either [that I die absolutely or not] and thus . . . a resigned despair and its resultant struggle."[20] It is precisely in the consciousness of life subject to time that man knows himself to be finite[21] and resists the legacy of his own finitude ("and waking struggles with the sea"). At the same time man struggles with truth, but within the framework of his speculation ("in dreams") since the concept of an absolute truth is not forced upon him by his existence, as the concept of death is.

It is not only death, however, which is inherent in existence, but the resistence to the absolute extinction of death as well. Consonant with Unamuno's "this our desire never to die is our immediate essence"[22] is Machado's portrait of the human spirit serving as its own bulwark against time and death:

> The soul conquers . . .
> the angel of death and the waters of forgetfulness.
>
> Its fortitude resists the siege of time as a strong
> bridge with dike withstands the river's blows;
> beneath, time bears its torrent thundering along,
> its murky water which unto the sea goes.
>
> Poet, the soul alone is anchor on the shore.[23]

Conscious that the course of life sweeps everything to its destruction, man is still able to remember ("The soul conquers . . . the waters of forgetfulness") and to hope ("conquers . . . the angel of death"). By daring to hope and by salvaging something of the past in memory ("Its fortitude resists the siege of time"), man clings to a sense of permanence, to that which holds firm against the siege of time. There is no defense against life's transiency, except the human spirit itself ("Poet, the soul alone is anchor on the shore").

But hope and memory are not the children of man's reason; rather they are dreams born of the encounter between understanding and uncertainty:

> I know not what
> divine poet
> wed to the bitterness
> of the eternal wheel
> the sweet harmony
> of water's dream
> and bound the eyes
> of the waterwheel's mule.
>
> But I know he was
> a poet divine;
> a heart with darkness
> and with knowledge full.[24]

That life is motion, the endlessly turning waterwheel, is tacitly acknowledged by one who creates another reality ("water's dream"). What man derives from the limited wisdom of human experience ("a heart with darkness / and with knowledge full") from which the dream is born, he unites to an awareness of temporality and the bitterness it begets. To recall the past and to speculate on the future requires an object which one first knows in the context of living ("with knowledge") and which in the context of time one recognizes to be absent or mysterious ("with darkness").

But when this dream is united to the present, it sings harmoniously of the continuity of life ("the sweet harmony / of water's dream"). Although the poet does not know precisely the manner in which this union takes place ("I know not what / divine poet . . ."), he acknowledges that the act confronts time with valor and seeks to transcend it ("But I know he was / a poet divine").

He who seeks truth, however, does not deceive himself with his dream. Continuity and change are coexistent and lead to an inevitable question:

> Which is true? The river
> which flows and leads
> where ship and sailor are
> themselves but waves of sea?
> Or perhaps this dream of mariner
> with his eternal anchor and his shore?[25]

Throughout his life this interplay of hope ("with his eternal anchor") and despair ("The river / which flows and leads / where ship and sailor are / themselves but waves of sea?") defines Machado's concept of the relation between life and truth. As Pierre Damangeat accurately observes in his essay on Machado as a poet of solitude: "His skepticism is not dogmatic: not at all 'a priori,' but a live doubt, the harassed faith of one who seeks himself or seeks his God, which amounts to the same thing."[26] In pursuing absolute truth, not in the abstract but consistently in a personal identification which he calls God, the poet seeks *for himself* a reconciliation between the temporality of life and the desire for permanence. His need for God springs from his own inherent need to transcend human limitations:

> I cannot chant, nor praise, nor should
> I wish, this Christ made of wood,
> but rather he who walked upon the sea.[27]

The biblical account of Christ walking on the water does not so much inspire the poet as correspond both directly and symbolically to his aspirations. To walk upon water is, physically, to transcend the laws of nature; and, symbolically, to overcome the limitations of finite existence which culminate in death for each man. Machado's image of Christ, like Unamuno's "Cristo de

Velázquez," emphasizes not the anguish of the Passion but the transcendence of death embodied in the act of dying itself. Since death is the lot of man, symbolically he is subject to the sea;[28] but if man attains the perfect truth to which he aspires, he too transcends death:

> Every man who journeys, walks,
> like Christ upon the sea.[29]

The journey described by "every man who journeys" is not identical with the image of man's life as a river, since the latter is swept along by a power outside itself, while one who walks is his own source of motion. Further, the river disappears into the sea, whereas here man is described as walking "*upon* the sea." Thus within the necessary flow of life to its end, the journey which man undertakes as an act of will is a rebellion, not against reaching the sea but against absorption in it. The phrase "like Christ" not only qualifies the road as supernatural but also provides the premise upon which its certainty rests: if, as the Bible affirms, Christ is both God and a human person who has overcome death, there exists infinite truth, toward which man can aspire and in which he can rise above the limitation of his own finitude.

Acceptance of this premise is typical of the Spanish peasant ("he who at his altars insults God") whom Machado portrays as affirming "God is a road upon the sea."[30] But faith was interpreted by most writers of the Generation of '98 as incompatible with their intellectual curiosity and their desire for perfect certainty and understanding. Hence they rejected the doctrinal assurances of immortality offered by religion. At the heart of each writer's ideas one finds, in greater or less degree, Unamuno's "I cannot know." Thus Machado's image of the road upon the sea suggests not only the transcending of finite limitations, but the futility of life as well:

All things change and all remain;
to change is our appointed way;
to journey making roads,
roads that on the sea we lay.[31]

Implicit in the paradox of the road upon the sea is the futility of human motion since the road is a purely subjective creation, brief and insubstantial as the wake which a boat momentarily cuts across the water. To continue this futile action is, however, imposed upon man by the terms of his existence ("to change is our appointed way"). Recognizing how ephemeral his path is, man cannot abandon it without surrendering his existence, and thus testifies to the irony of life.

The image itself is ironic and contradictory. A road upon the sea suggests the transcendence implicit in Christ's walking upon the water precisely because it is paradoxical: it defies the fact that men sink into the sea. But paradox also contains a sense of hopelessness: such a road is, in itself, poor and vague and fleeting.

The balance between the two aspects of the image, the one hopeful and creative, the other despairing and destructive, is the same as the chiaroscuro of life, at once fleeting and enduring:

But though unto unknown sea it flows,
life also must as the fountain be
whose water from the stone arose
and there repeats your name eternally![32]

Clinging to love and to the inherently stable image of the stone fountain, the poet possesses something which is not only alive but eternal. But it is a personal and feeble possession, for the affirmation of being ("life also must as the fountain be") is encompassed by the image of life destined for its end ("unto unknown sea it flows"). To see in the human process of becoming simultaneous destruction and genesis requires, as Machado acknowledges, an act of faith:

> Oh water good, land's life sew
> as you go.
> Oh you who, drop by drop, are
> fountain by fountain, river by river born
> as this time of boredom, forlorn,
> and rushing goes into the sea afar,
> with all things desiring to be,
> all that hopes to
> flower free
> beneath spring's sun anew,
> kindly be
> that on the morrow
> early grain will your life's borrow,
> as flesh puts on its glow and field its greenery;
> yet more be: reason, madness too
> and bitterness of who
> wishes and cannot achieve:
> to believe, believe and believe.[33]

Of life hurrying to its end ("rushing . . . into the sea afar"), he begs a regeneration ("Land's life sew / as you go"), like nature's renaissance. In this regeneration life as the source and subject of time is no longer manifest in the distinct aspects of existence. The water, which is a source, is identical with the river in its journey to the sea. At the same time this water in flight is creative. Herein lies the paradoxical example ("reason"), irrational ("madness too") and therefore always uncertain ("and bitterness"), for one who desires intensely—an intensity emphasized by the repetition—but is unable to believe.

Machado's desire to believe is essentially a desire to understand, for the hope which he perceives in death is that of transcending the temporal limitations of his own personality. Death inspires terror, he says in a letter to Unamuno, if it confirms finally and absolutely these limitations.[34] This enigma of death or self-realization:

> To die . . . To fall, a drop
> from the sea into sea immense?
> Or to be what I have never been:
> one . . . ?[35]

is the fundamental issue in man's dialogue wtih time. Ultimately Machado confronts the reality of time with the ephemeral reality of his hope and asks "What is it to die; is it not, perhaps, to possess truth?"

All of Machado's life is oriented toward the attainment of truth. Even as he accepts and employs the conventional image of man upon the road of life, he rejects the notion that any fixed road exists since man understands neither where his journey will end nor the terrain through which he must pass. Constrained to proceed through and by the circumstances of life, he possesses no path save that which his own journey describes, step by step. If this is true of every life, whatever its goal, then the search for absolute truth, by one who is not certain that his goal exists, must be the most nebulous of all journeys. Nevertheless, fully cognizant of the obscure and equivocal character of his search, Machado remains dedicated to this ideal.

In using the traditional metaphor of life's road, the poet acknowledges that all men are traveling. Thus, for example, death is awaited by one who is said to be seated at the side of the road.[36] He does not, however, envision a smooth, well-charted path stretching before the traveler. One who assumes that, having sallied forth into existence, he is now upon a true highway to a definite end, is deceiving himself, and, the poet believes, should be disillusioned:

Traveler, your footsteps are
the road and nothing more.
Traveler, there is no road,
you make a road in traveling.
Traveling you make a road
and upon your gazing back
appears the path which
ne'er again is to be trod.
Traveler, there is no road.
Nought but a wake upon the sea.[37]

That the poet addresses himself to a traveler—Spanish: *caminante*—implies a journey and a road (*camino*) where the traveler's footsteps already provide visible evidence of the progress involved. But the security in these assumptions is immediately rejected as an illusion, both in an individual reference ("*your* footsteps are the road") and as an absolute principle ("there is no road"). And since the traveler is concerned both with the past—the road traversed—and with the future—the road still to be trod—the poet's denial applies to his entire life. Thus there is simultaneously revealed to him the true character of his former experiences and the obligation implicit in life to continue making one's uncertain way. Affirming this obligation, Machado repeats his declaration, now inverted to emphasize the manner in which the road can acquire reality: "*Traveling* you make a road." Not even on this road, however, does the traveler find consolation since his own existence continues to drive him toward an unknown future, while memories only intensify his sense of privation. Behind him there is a real path, but time has erected a transparent barrier between the past and the present through which only visions pass ("and upon your gazing back / appears the path which / ne'er again is to be trod"). The poet's denial is doubly justified: neither past nor future truly comforts or assures man as he continues his transitory journey ("a wake upon the sea") through the vast and engulfing unknown.

Constrained by life to journey and to chart his own course, the poet determines that his shall be a purposeful road, that it shall be a search for truth, involving every facet of his being. Even as a young man he saw a creative aspect in the act of living: "I have traveled many roads / opened many paths."[38] Employing roads to indicate both physical journeys and previous experience, he implies that the knowledge gained is the result of a personal effort.[39] Reflecting upon his life in retrospect, he acknowledges not only the active but also the subjective character of his endeavor: "I have been, don Ramón, a traveler in dreams upon a harsh road."[40]

"I have been . . . a traveler *in dreams*. . . ." If there is no real road to travel, then from the reality of the physical world, from the memory of past experiences, and from hopes and desires, one must conceive one's own road, as in a dream. For dreams fuse fact and illusion, blur the temporal distinctions which our consciousness makes, so that the past can be projected into the future, and the future represented as present; and belong intimately to the dreamer, involving, but not wholly determined by, his intellect. The personality of each dream, however, in spite of these common qualities, is unique, since into it enter senses, emotions, mind and will, which are themselves constantly changing. Thus each dream-road has a common ancestry in the search for truth and a particular orientation, as, for example, the understanding of sorrow:

> I, on roads of afternoon, go
> dreaming. Golden are
> the hills, the pines a green row,
> the oaks dust-covered, spare.
> Where might this path bend?

I go singing along my way
the length entire of road and day,
—the afternoon draws to its end—.
In my heart once I bore
the spine of a passion driven deep;
one day from my heart I tore
it, now I neither feel nor weep.

Then a moment all the field
mute and shadowed stood,
lost in thought. As a bell, pealed
the wind amidst the wood.

The afternoon darker grows
and the wandering road
grows faint as day grows cold
until the path scarcely shows.

I make my song again:
Sharp, golden spiny knife
would that your keen pain
might my heart awake to life.[41]

A vehicle for the dreaming poet, this road belongs to both a physical and a spiritual landscape. The poem's physical setting is located in space: "Golden are the hills . . .," etc., and in time: "roads of afternoon," with an oblique reference to the clarity of the day—since the hills are gilded, the sun is shining. As a spiritual characterization "roads of afternoon" imply that the journey is a culmination.[42] As the afternoon declines, life too moves on, reawakening the memory of a past sorrow ("In my heart once I bore . . .") and, thus, both an awareness of temporal contrast ("now I neither feel nor weep") and a realization that sorrow gives meaning to life. Dreaming, one does not necessarily know where his path will lead nor is one able to arrest permanently time's flight. But in the dreamer's moment of understanding, life pauses ("Then a moment all the field / mute and shadowed stood / lost in thought"); the dream briefly transcends reality.

To journey in a dream is, moreover, not only to grasp the importance of sorrow and to understand the past, but also to project one's memories into the future:

> Over the bitter earth
> a dream lays labyrinthine
> roads, torturous parks,
> parks in flower, in shadow and in silence wrapt,
>
> deep crypts, ladders over stars,
> scene of hope and memory.
> Figures that pass and smile,
> —melancholy toys of former times—;
>
> images beloved
> at the flowered turning of the road
> and pale chimeras
> that afar describe a road . . .[43]

In the harsh world where there are no roads ("the bitter earth"), the dream provides a path which transcends reality, contrasts with the bitterness of the world, and is born as a reaction against that bitterness. Actually here, as in "I, on roads of afternoon, go / dreaming," the dream reveals not a single road but various roads. Both poems, however, treat these roads as a single entity. The poet is not concerned with pointing out the differences between one dream-road and another, but rather with acknowledging that no dream provides an absolute answer to all man's questions nor a single satisfaction for all his needs. Each dream opens many avenues, infinitely multiplied by the many dreams of numberless dreamers.

Nor is the dream-road a smooth, straight path. Just as he who travels in life's afternoon does not see his journey's end (and asks "Where might this path bend?"), one who walks over the bitter earth treads a twisting path ("labyrinthine / roads, torturous paths"). And although the dreamer is permitted a vision of life, time and his own understanding obscure the images which pass before him ("parks . . . in shadow and in silence wrapt"), images which are unable to pierce his solitude and speak to him. The past and the future appear to him as human copies of reality ("scenes of hope and memory"), visible but mute representations of his memories and hopes. Between the poet and his vision lies an expanse of years in which voices fade and are lost. Communication is a pathetic effort to span this temporal distance ("Figures that pass and smile / —melancholy toys of former times—"). But, although silent and distant, these images fuse memories and hopes and thereby impart to the future the substantial form of the past. Thus, as the poet journeys in his dream, the figures of his memories become images of life and beauty awaiting him ("images beloved / at the flowered turning of the road"). Dreaming still, he discerns a road, product of his own fancy, which will carry him into that distant time ("and pale chimeras / that afar describe a road . . .").

This road in dreams is indeed a chimera. And yet, in a world of uncertainties and limitations, how, except by imagination and by the effort of one's own will, is one to journey at all? Whoever acknowledges the futility of life's journey ("To journey making roads / roads which on the sea we lay"), yet resists despair with a suggestion of transcendence ("Every man who journeys, walks / as Christ upon the sea"),[44] sees life shadowed by uncertainty where the dream fades:

> The red sun of a dream now appears in the West.
> Light in dreams. Do you, pilgrim, not fear?
> Beyond the green plain on the flowered crest
> perhaps the end of your road is near.[45]

If the journey does end in the midst of abundance and vitality, then the aspirations implied by the characterization *pilgrim* are all realized. For a pilgrim is both a stranger in his surroundings and a seeker. But to be, as the Spanish text specifies, an errant pilgrim *(andante peregrino)* is to seek without a clear concept of one's goal or the certainty of attaining it. Thus if this pilgrim encounters life at his search's end, his is not merely an act of achieving, but also one of defining his desire and of proving its existence. Nothing, of course, is actually defined or proved, since attainment ("the end of your road") is always circumscribed by doubt ("perhaps the end of your road is near").

The journey's end remains doubtful, so that when, after the poem on Abel Martín's death, Machado concludes the *Cancionero apócrifo* with "Otro clima" (Another Place or Another Country), he neither affirms life nor despairs, but continues to question:

Oh, chambers of time and galleries
of the soul! how bare!
said the poet: From days clear as these
pass mute shadows rare.
The song of former hours now is gone
such as I sang in shelter rimmed;
time bears its sequences of dawn
each with its retinue of stars bedimmed.
Does a world die? Or is there born
another world? Is this marine
belly of the globe now worn
by a new ship whose diamond wake is seen?
Keel to the sun lies the old ship forlorn?
Is the world conceived in sin and pain,
this world of labor and fatigue absurd,
a good world to be saved again?
Again! May it please God to speak that word.

Then ceased the poet, the solitary man, to speak
because the air of stiffened sky
his fine Stradivarius made faint, made weak
and all his hearing had drained dry.
From the peak he saw the empty plain
with shadow marked of giants, shields in hand
and in the ocean's green crash strain
the naked torsos of slaves upon the sand.
And then a nihil writ in flame and spark
beyond the murky woodland showed
itself in stolid granite stark
and in the mountain far, the ribbon of a road.[46]

As the poem proceeds, constantly growing in intensity, from a universalized statement about life through a series of questions into the ultimate fate of all existence, to a personal encounter with death, its world becomes one of metaphor and fantastic images. Death has no common language with man. We speak from our experiences, and we have no experience of death from which to draw the vocabulary, the images or the accepted terminology with which to clothe our ideas. But the poet strives, in spite of the limitations of language, to shape images which will both express a progressive consciousness of death and communicate that consciousness. His point of departure, therefore, is an awareness he shares with other men: time erases our recollections, silences yesterday's voices, and follows each dawn with night. Facing endless night, he perceives that here all experience and all searching are to be reborn or to be extinguished. The world lives for him in his knowledge of it; thus, in asking "Does a world Die? Or is there born / another world?" he seeks to know his own fate. Journeying, he has sought truth; in the metaphor of the ship he considers that search. Beyond death, one may proceed with understanding (". . . a new ship whose diamond wake is seen?") or in death all journeying may end, the ship upturned upon the shore ("Keel to the sun lies the old ship forlorn?"). Is this world of sorrow and limitations the only world, he asks, or is there another—"a good world to be saved again?"

And death's answer is itself a limitation ("the air of stiffened sky / his fine Stradivarius made faint, made weak / and all his hearing had drained dry"). All that remains is a vision of unknown fears grown monstrous in the proximity of death and of the fears he has understood—the loss of everything, even his personality, and the final surrender to time—embodied in the image of the headless slaves in the livid sea. But even as each image prepares for and confirms the permanent sunset ("a nihil writ in flame and spark . . . in stolid granite stark"), there remains the glimmer of a road in the distance. If it is a real road, then the poet is still journeying, for he sees in personal extinction the annihilation of *all* reality; the continuity of any image is dependent upon his own continuity. Yet this may be no more than a last illusion, a deceptive reflection of the nihil writ in flame. In a finite world, enclosed by time, the dream search and its implicit road are the only eternals. They are the links between truth desired and doubt acknowledged.

The ultimate bond between man and nature is change, seen not as a single relationship but as a series of associations between the multiple temporal conditions of the world and the individual temporal experience of man. It is true both that change in nature is slower than human change and that it is swifter. When Gerardo Diego observes in Machado's poetry a *tempo lento*[47] he is, in effect, describing the rapport between poetic rhythm and the movement which Juan de Mairena finds "in nature's symphony [in which] the poet senses rhythms different from that of his own pulse and generally slower."[48] Mountains, sea, rivers and the general contours of the landscape may encompass generations of men in their evolution. At the same time, as the days and the seasons pass, each individual life witnesses myriad cycles in nature. Identifying personal and historical experiences with nature, the poet realizes a temporal condensation in which he, as Bousoño notes, "perceives immediately or almost immediately a transformation which [in the world] occurs only over a much longer temporal span."[49] In addition, these cycles indicate a reality in which culmination and decline suggest a new beginning. But man knows only one temporal condition intimately: life consuming itself. A human renaissance, like the dawn or the spring, is the object of faith, or hope, or speculation.

As he journeys upon the road of his own creation, accompanied by a vision of the road already traveled, and motivated by a desire for absolute truth, perhaps to be attained at the journey's end, Machado sees life in the present both as completion and as a motive for hope. A product of circumstances which now endure only as memory, his present is an afternoon where dreams are born and where, dreaming, he awaits the dawn. But the objects of memory and hope are absent and, therefore, shadowed, so that the poet understands everything imperfectly. There is something unknown in all of life, and in the end of life there is nothing but enigma.

In describing our road as essentially nascent and his own life as a constant search, Machado implies that man always finds himself at a moment of beginning and, therefore, directed toward the future. In order to speak about the future, however, unknown and formless, the poet must have recourse to the past, with its concrete physical associations. Thus even his hopes force him to recognize that life is a product and a recapitulation of previous experiences.

It is always late (*tarde*); memory, journey, hope and dreams fuse in the afternoon (*la tarde*) of his life. Machado's critics, in particular Julián Marías,[50] have pointed out his rapport with Azorín in the treatment of the Castilian landscape and the concrete commonplace. This is not, however, the only similarity between them. Both Machado's first book, *Soledades,* and the triology in which Martínez Ruiz creates Azorín are dominated by scenes set in the afternoon and by the authors' recollections of and meditations upon the past. Yet both were written by young men. Machado at twenty-eight[51] called himself an old traveler who had wandered along many paths, who grieved for past loves and recalled past sorrows. Only thirty, Azorín reflected "this idea that it is always late has been the central concern of my life." It is precisely their common belief—that man is defined by his relationship to tangible objects[52] and that human understanding is, therefore, bound to sensory reality—which underlies their conclusion: it is always late. Every temporal description is relative: we can define the present only in terms of other specific moments in time. And if the past alone is understood, however imperfectly, then our present is a climax and a limit upon our knowledge.

Tangible things as means of communicating with the past have already appeared in the image of stone fountains. Similarly lemon trees, patios and plazas evoke Seville, as, later in Machado's life, memories of Soria persist in her mountains and craggy hillsides, her dusty oak groves and tenacious herbs. The afternoon itself recalls other afternoons, for the only continuity completely immune to change is time itself. Contemplating the changing and the enduring world, the poet concludes: "Everything comes and everything passes. / Nothing is eternal."[53] Even man's efforts in stone and marble to overcome corruptibility eventually mock him. Spain's yesterday remains, ironically, in the crumbling stone of her old cities and ruined castles: Soira "with her warrior's fort . . . in ruins, decay / with her rotted tumbling walls, / and her time-despoiled halls."[54] And the most creative of human emotions, love, is merely a transient possession: "It was a day / (tic-toc, tic-toc) that passed, / and that which I most loved / death bore it away."[55] Nor is nature entirely invulnerable: a dying tree, the flowers fallen or about to fall, and the yellowed leaves suggest the finality of all life. Time is an endless monotony of days, but each day can be said to die: "The afternoon is dying / like a humble hearth that at last burns out."[56]

Yet the poet remembers all these things: his youth, his love, his sorrows, and because of his memories the past is not dead but absent:

> . . . . It is a bright afternoon,
> almost spring . . . .
> and alone I stand in the silent patio
> seeking an old illusion, familiar to me,
> some shadow on the white stone wall,
> some memory laid upon the threshold there
> of the sleepy fountain . . . .
>
> . . . . .
>
> And in the air of afternoon there floats
> a scent of absence which
> to the luminous soul says: never,
> but to the heart cries: hope.[57]

The hard physical reality of the patio walls and the stone fountain occasions memory. Dimensionless, the images recollected are perceptible only as shadows upon the visible world ("some shadow on the white stone wall") and communicate with the poet through the most tenuous of sensory experiences ("a scent of absence"). Machado realized, years before he read Bergson, that memories dwell on the boundary between sense—the object perceived—and will—the effort to recall. Thus, although the poet is able to contact the past in solid stone images, memories themselves are but tenuous replicas of sense impressions, shadows, echoes, scents. He is able to recall his beloved because of a subtle accord between the scent of her hair and the aroma of a rose which opened in his rose garden:

> Then as a flame the brilliance burst of your hair
> which in verses he called waves of golden tone;
> appeared anew because the same scent wafted there
> and he withdrew in silence awhile to weep alone.[58]

Just as this particular memory recalls both life and the grief of loneliness, every awareness of the past reveals to the poet the finality of loss ("to the luminous soul says: never") and simultaneously creates a new illusion of possession and source of hope ("but to the heart cries: hope"). Thus, hoping, he searches for life in finality itself, in the light of fading day:

> The land is bare
> and the soul at the pale horizon howls
> like a hungry wolf. What do you seek,
> poet, in the West?
> A few stiff trees grow dark;
> and in the distant mountains are
> touches of gold and blood. The sun has died. What
> do you seek, poet, in the West?[59]

In the midst of the deprivation of the physical world, man is utterly possessionles and reaches out in his need to the last echoes of light retreating from him. He cannot check its movement: the light inches gradually away into the distance, leaving the motionless trees in darkness. Time's presence is felt in this progressive extinction of all illumination, culminating in "the sun has died." But the last traces of the sun do not completely imply destruction: "in the distant mountains are / touches of gold and blood." Through these attributes of the sunset as a spiritual reality, the poet acknowledges that the day's consummation is death ("blood") but also senses in the dying light something durable and of intrinsic value ("gold"). Thus, even after the sun has died and the poet stands in complete darkness, he continues to search ("What do you seek, poet. . . .?"), not turning his eyes with certainty to the east in expectation of tomorrow's sun, but rather seeking dawn where the memory of day hovers ("in the West"). The light fleeing is his only tangible contact with the desired dawn:

> In the afternoon which broad as boredom is and clear,
> when the torrid summer more mellow its blows does reign,
> the fantasy of my grave dream was copied here
> in theory by countless shadows raised above the plain.
>
> The glory of the West a purple mirror seems,
> crystal forged of flame which all its dreams
> unto infinity across the wide plain has drawn,
> and I felt my sonorous footfall tread
> echo afar in western sky blood-red
> and then beyond, discerned the joyous song of dawn.[60]

From present afternoon to future dawn is not, in this poem, a simple space of hours. It is evident that these two periods of time are mutually exclusive: with the passage of time one is obliged to surrender what was formerly the present, accepting another present in its place. But here the poet, while still in the afternoon watching the sunset, is able to perceive the dawn, an image superimposed upon the afternoon but regarded as future ("then beyond"). Moreover, this is no pale ghost, but a vital reality ("the joyous song of dawn"). Being formless, the future owes its substance, as well as its existence and vitality, both to nature and to the poet: dawn is the offspring of the landscape and the dream. That which begins as a relationship between man and his surroundings ("the fantasy of my grave dream was copied here / in theory by countless shadows raised above the plain"), becomes a commingling of physical and spiritual properties. The sunset is a mirror, a reflection of the day and hence a distant memory of dawn. In addition, the world in which the sun now sets is described as old, the constant before which the day's cycle is endlessly repeated: nature both remembers and is capable of another dawn. Dreaming, the poet transforms this capability into actuality. It is his dream which the growing shadows spread over the world, and his animate reality which echoes in the dying day ("I felt my sonorous footfall tread / echo afar in western sky"). Life and the dream transcend mortality and time; the poet both hears and sees a future superior to the present: joyful as opposed to boring, lyrical as opposed to the sonorous footfall, white and innocent as opposed to the crystal forged of flame and the blood-red sky. Memory becomes creative when interpreted subjectively, capable of evoking a vital impression of the future: "In all memory, what matters is the gift of evoking dreams."[61]

Within a dream, time can be altered according to one's desires: "I dreamed again of absence and distance garbed now in tunics of the dawn."[62] That which is denied in reality and recognized as absent can be recreated as future. One can, in effect, possess anything in a dream, although the possession is an illusion:

> Last night as I slept
> I dreamed—illusion blessed!
> —that a fountain flowed
> within my heart.
> I said: why, hidden
> water, do you come to me,
> source of a new life,
> wherein I never drank?
>
> Last night as I slept
> I dreamed—illusion blessed!
> that I had a beehive
> within my heart

and these golden bees
made therein
from my old bitterness
honey sweet and combs for it.

Last night as I slept
I dreamed—illusion blessed!
that a burning sun
in my heart shone.

Burning as it glowed
with the red fire of the hearth,
as a sun which gave light
but which also sired tears.

Last night as I slept
I dreamed—illusion blessed!
—that it was God I held
there within my heart.[63]

Prefacing each image is the affirmation of its dependence upon the dream and the bitter awareness that each is, in fact, an illusion. Nevertheless, the dream vision is welcome ("illusion blessed") since it communicates to the poet a principle of life (water: "source of a new life"); a source of productive activity (the transforming labor of bees); light to give warmth and illumination; a sense of anguish to intensify and define human existence; and God or absolute and certain truth. Each possession, although ultimately fathered by the dream, flows also from the dream preceding it. It is the new life provided by the fountain which makes possible an intimate renaissance, the transformation of old sorrows, where life is illumined with a twofold meaning: understanding and grief. This dream wisdom, similar to Unamuno's tragic sense of life, leads to the attainment of truth, identified as God, a truth immutable and self-sufficient. But it is a dream.

If truth does exist, it will not be found in dreams but in the meeting of conscious and unconscious reality: in the act of waking. A particular truth would be revealed in the banishing of a particular illusion and absolute truth, if attainable, in purging all deception and limitation from life. And since living is circumscribed by limitations, the transcending of life is, perhaps, the attainment of understanding.

The deception inherent in total dependence upon memory is countered by the dawn of a vital actuality: "Singers, awake: / let the echoes cease / the voices begin."[64] The mystery of life and death, however, is not so easily resolved: "Between living and dreaming / lies a third possibility. / Guess."[65] This is the problem the poet cannot escape: "Beyond living and dreaming / lies that which matters more: / to wake."[66] Dreams dissolve and life ends; therefore that which lies beyond them both, death, is of ultimate importance. For the resolution of this mystery, the poet believes, every man must pursue his own solution. To acknowledge that which inevitably terminates life is not necessarily to possess, between the necessity of living and the illusion of dreaming, an insight into the meaning of death. It may be that man must resign himself to utter extinction or that religious belief in a life after death provides the true explanation. When the poet offers only the enigmatic advice—"Guess."—he is not playing a game with his reader or with himself; he himself does not know the solution to the riddle.

Mystery lurks wherever the poet seeks to comprehend himself or that which transcends his existence. All his knowledge is obscured by memories, by hopes, and by uncertainty: everything which he perceives is shadowed. Thus, striving to evoke the past, he describes himself as "seeking an old, candid illusion: / some shadows on the white wall cast, / some memory."[67]

Similarly, the memory of Soria is represented as a physical shadow over the landscape of the present, Baeza, obscuring that present:

> How often have you erased for me,
> land of ashes, the memory
> of verdant lemon trees
> with the dead shade of your black oaks![68]

But the same shadow of memory is also a source of grief because it increases the poet's consciousness of the lost reality. Thinking of his dead wife he finds himself "alone with my shadow and my grief."[69] And yet the shadow which endures when the reality has fled is, like grief itself, good:

> Water is good as is our thirst.
> Good the shadow and so the sun.
> The honey of rosemary flower made
> as the honey of unflowering field.[70]

In the three facets of this single vision, one image awaits, suggests the existence of, and justifies its own worth in terms of the other. The desire for life is both a hope that life can be attained and an affirmation that the attainment is possible, since the desire supposes some prior knowledge of that which satisfies thirst. Thus, as motivation and as assurance, it merits esteem. Similarly, shadow, which is uncertain, by nature seeks the certain; indicates that this illumination does exist, since shadow is impossible without light; and motivates those who are dissatisfied with the limitations of an obscured understanding to seek a perfect or certain light. So too a barren field both awaits spring and recalls the presence of flowers in the honey made from them. As the flowers endure transformed, life enobles its own transient circumstances, creating from momentary beauty and joys, memories and hopes.

That man aspires to unshadowed understanding, of course, does not mean that he will or can attain this. At the end of a life dedicated to seeking an eternal dawn, the poet, in the person of Abel Martín, acknowledges that the object of his search can only be found—if, indeed, it does exist—outside the temporal frame of life:

> And then he saw his sacred muse
> standing by his bed in mourning clad,
> the lady of his paths, obtuse,
> impossible to love, yet ever he had
> loved. Lady, to her Abel did declare,
> in thirst your hidden face to see
> I thought toward dawn my life to bear
> until that hour when life should cease in me.
> But now I know that you are not as I believed.
> Yet I should like to look on you and make
> my thanks who long companionship of you received:
> your cold disdain. On Martin now
> death wished to smile and knew not how.[71]

This search ("toward dawn my life to bear") has motivated his life, remaining ever desired but ever illusive. The proximity of death, however, brings recognition: the desired truth does not belong to a reality limited by time ("now I know that you are not as I believed"). Yet this objective, however poorly understood, had sustained the poet ("I should like . . . [to] make / my thanks who long companionship of you received") and, therefore, has been a benevolent companion, good in the sense in which shadow, thirst and barren fields are good. This encounter with death may be a prelude to the attainment of true wisdom, although the poet is not certain, and death, inasmuch as she is mystery and impassivity, cannot tell him ("On Martin now / death wished to smile and knew not how.").

The experience of death is an encounter with shadows:

And must sun from new day erased be?
Abel reached out his hand
toward that red lit dome
that is warm dawn o'er summer land
come to the balcony of his ancient home.
Blind, he sought the light he could not see.
Then unto his cold lips, calm and still,
the glass of shadow he
lifted up—of pure shadow only—full.[72]

In attempting to identify throughout Machado's poetry a philosophy consonant with that of Heidegger, Serrano Poncela interprets the repeated references to death as the poet's effort to resign himself to absolute extinction and the expression "pure shadow" as the actual act of resignation to a fate which completes the circle of life in perfect limitation.[73] In the last decade of his life, Machado increasingly questions the existence of a reality superior to that relative and changing world which man knows and which he calls reality. It is not possible, however, to apply this attitude freely to every poem mentioning death, nor to conclude that the poet accepted absolute finitude[74] as the ultimate answer to his question: "What is it to die?" (personal as opposed to "What is death?"). One cannot, for example, ignore the explicit expressions of hope in his letters to Unamuno, both referring to his wife: "Sometimes I have such hope. . . . In short, she lives in me more than ever and sometimes I firmly believe I shall be reunited with her,"[75] and to all men: "We sleep? Very well, and we dream. But we must also wake. We must hope, doubt with faith."[76] The problem has a poetic form:

To die. . . . To fall, a drop
from the sea into sea immense?
Or to be what I have never been,
one, without shadow now or dream,
a lone man continuing without
road or mirror reflecting him?[77]

But this statement cannot be reconciled with this theory of resignation. One might interpret "to be what I have never been, one" as absolute finitude, were it not for the additional description "a lone man *continuing*," which is hardly indicative of finality.

The rapport between Heidegger and Machado consists in their recognition of human anguish as "a vision of the totality of our existence and a reflection on its fulfillment and end: death."[78] *End* is not, however, as Serrano Poncela himself points out, identical with absolute finitude since it does not define human nature but only identifies its temporal limit.

Unseeing, still the poet seeks a light; enveloped in shadow, he does not know if death extinguishes all light. The shadow itself is not a solution, for in death one will possess light or nothing. The glass of life is drained of its mystery ("the glass of shadow he / lifted up—of pure shadow only—full") as the poet penetrates death to discover the answer so long desired.

This is the final culmination toward which all of life's afternoons have transported the poet. Seeking dawn in fading sunset, in memory, in a dream, and in waking from the dream, he recognizes that his search will be ended only when time has ceased to exist. Shadows of recollection, of desire, and of doubt can be dispersed only upon encountering pure shadow at life's temporal limit. Perhaps they have concealed from the poet only the void awaiting him. Yet, unseeing, he continues to seek the light ("Blind, he sought the light he could not see."); unknowing, he does not abandon his hope.

Machado—poet of afternoons, of sunsets and the hope of dawn—is above all a poet of spring: the land awaiting, cold March days in Soria with the first flowers in the land and the gradual realization of the season's fullness: "In the uplands / of the Duero's bank, spring comes late / but how lovely is she when she comes."[79] Scenes of winter are few, although winter dominates Soria during at least five months of the year. But in Machado's vision the world coming to be and in flower prevails because it is an affirmation of life. The seasons' cycle has more personal associations for him than that of the day, since afternoon and dawn are essentially intangible although visible, while spring is physically present in each particular of the transformed landscape. Images of a familiar, transformed countryside presage a similar transformation of spiritual reality.

Sometimes there is beauty to be found in autumn, but it is a doomed beauty, destined for imminent destruction; in other years there is only barrenness, the inheritance of a dry summer. Spring, on the other hand, is inherently benevolent. Its flowers evoke youthful innocence, joy and love; its fields and trees recover their lost beauty and manifest renascent life. In the midst of this renaissance, new hopes are born: a vision of Leonor and a dream of eternal spring.

Such hopes are not easily sustained in autumn when all nature echoes the temporal limits of life. Unlike the day, which departs in brilliance and leaves images of light which suggest a new dawn, the year dies in somber slowness, in dry leaves and the falling petals of flowers: "while ashen clouds pass / shadowing the field / the dry pastures / and the gray olive groves."[80] In this season memories are engulfed in a sense of loss; the poet, wandering among the dry elms rattling in the wind, cries out of an intense awareness of his solitude: "I can no longer walk with her [Leonor]."[81] Through a similar landscape passes the tragic figure of the village idiot "shouting in the musty, tattered afternoon / of a fruitless autumn, in the sterile / rotted land."[82] For nature, as for the idiot, this particular afternoon's wretchedness represents an existence entirely consumed by misery. The idiot's madness rises out of a collection of evils—"poor vices, / miserable virtues and tasks / of bored fops and the wickedness of lazy merchants,"[83]—just as the fruitless autumn is a product of summer's drought and withered fields.

Even when there are evidences of life in nature, the proximity of death haunts the autumnal scene:

> The trees have
> green leaves still
> but a musty green it is
> of stunted fronds.
> The wind shakes a few
> yellow leaves.[84]

Although life endures, it is already late ("green leaves *still*"), and decay has begun its destruction ("but a musty green . . . of stunted fronds"). A few dead leaves prophesy the fate awaiting all nature. In spite of this emphasis upon death, the poet is, on occasion, able to preserve, as he and the year mature, the innocence of spring and youth:

> While pass the shadows of a holy love, I this day
> wish to place a dulcet ode upon my ancient music stand.
> I shall recall the notes which severe organs play
> while fragrant sighs the fife in April's hand.
>
> Autumnal apples rich shall ripened be their scent,
> the myrrh and incense of their odor make a chant
> and rose groves all their fresh perfume have spent
> beneath the shadowed peace that a garden's blossoms grant.
>
> To grave and slow accord that melody and scene unite,
> the lone and aged and noble reason of my prayer
> shall soar as graceful dove and rise in flight
> and this white word shall unto the altar high repair.[85]

Maturing, both nature and the poet are conscious of the memory, respectively, of April and of a former love. It is the awareness of time passing which motivates the poet and directs his song. The involvement of scent and sound, the opulence of the images—reminiscent of Valle-Inclán's *Sonatas* or of Keats's "St.

Agnes' Eve" and indicative of *modernista* influence in this poem —the self-consciously romantic conceits ("the fife in April's hand"), the baroque transformations of syntax, and the psalmodic tone of the entire poem imply that maturity, human and natural, is an elaboration and intensification, even a stylization, of youth. From this autumnal world with its rich aromas and its even, stately rhythms—Al grá-ve‿a-cór-de lén-to de mú-si-cá y‿a-ró-ma, / la só-la‿y vié-ja‿y nó-ble ra-zón de mí re-zár—arises a song which preserves the innocence and sacredness of youth.

Spring is, for Machado, preeminently the season of nascent innocence to which his memories and desires, seeking their own rebirth, address themselves. Spiritually the Sorian countryside lies between the abundant, fertile fields of Andalusia and the craggy, eternally arid meseta that runs south from the Guadarrama to Toledo. While winter still clings to the land, April leaves the first flowers in the brambles and the herbs hidden among rocks, the first violets and white daisies. For the poet these few, fragile blossoms represent his own tenuous hopes and the spirit of Soria, with its capacity for life slowly, almost imperceptively, realized:

I

The land of Soria arid is and cold.
Throughout the hills and peaks,
green meadows, ashen cliffs,
passes by the spring
leaving among the fragrant herbs
its daisies diminutive and white.

But the land does not revive; the fields sleep.
As April comes, snow covers still
Moncayo's slopes;
the traveler wraps his scarf
about his neck and mouth while shepherds
go ensconced in their long capes.

II

In the farm lands,
as scraps of beige-toned cloth,
the little garden where Merinos graze
among the dusty peaks, is sown
the joyful dream of an Arcadia young.

Amid the distant poplars, the road along,
stiff the branches seem to fade
into one green mist—of new leaves made—
and in the valley hedge and nitch
the brambles white blossoms now put forth
and perfumed violets appear.[86]

In the first and second stanzas there is scarcely a hint of spring among the images which elaborate the opening description: "The land of Soria arid is and cold." Only the diminutive white daisies affront winter: whiteness contrasting with the grey rocks; their smallness with the massive peak of Moncayo; their delicacy with the biting chill which forces even men accustomed to the cold to protect themselves in warm clothing. From this beginning, life reaches out through the countryside, opening patches of arable land; stirring dreams of idyllic beauty and abundance; multiplying itself as it progresses in the new foliage, vaguely perceptive, and in flowers, enchanting first with color, then with scent.

This growing aura of spring unquestionably originates in the image of the white daisies, which together with a few other early spring flowers, also white, repeatedly summarize for Machado the first evidence of rebirth. When the Castilian country girl dreams in her snowbound house of the coming spring, she imagines the vitality of the season in which she will take part ("in the green meadows / she will run with other girls") and the sun-blessed countryside visualized in a single image: "the blue and golden days / when white daisies grow."[87] Both the girl and the daisies are young, petite, vital. The innocence and daintiness frequently identified with the color white are accentuated by associating the life of the little girl with the natural life of the flowers.

In whiteness, the poet sees not only youthful innocence but also joy:

> The spring has come,
> ¡White hosonnas of
> the brambles now appear![88]

That the Spanish flowering brambles are white need be no more than a descriptive observation. But in the spring "white hosonnas" suggests the joyful spirit of Easter.

This beauty is also a reflection of love, both erotic and sublimated. Whoever asks of his beloved, "has the field for you donned this youthful attire?,"[89] sees the season's first flowers in the world transformed by love. The poet's emotion may also be directed toward the landscape itself. His vision of spring extending through the countryside along the Duero is based on the image of "some humble flower, blue or white born amid the herbs,"[90] and produces an immediate personal response to the spiritual character of the scene: "Beauty of the scarcely flowered field and mystic spring!" Alone in the poor, cold land, the flower's solitude and purity suggest the mystic quality of spring, which together with youth, innocence, joy and love describes the season's benevolence.

Memories arise in the poet's heart and beget dreams and hopes:

> Spring gently the
> tree grove kissed
> and green growth was
> as a green mist.

The clouds floated o'er
the young field and lane.
I saw in trembling branches
the fresh April rain.

Beneath the flowering tree
bowed with blossoms above
I recalled that I had damned
my youth devoid of love.

Now, midway in my life
I pause to think anew:
Youth I never lived,
would I might dream again of you![91]

Memories of a youth without love are evoked through an amorous image in nature: "Spring . . . the tree grove / kissed." Because the season's creative spirit, so long desired, has transformed the world, the poet seeks to possess once more his own dead past so that his nostalgic desires may perhaps be fulfilled. "In reality, when we contemplate the past," writes Juan de Mairena, "it is easy to find in it a culmination of hopes—not realized, but not lost either—, a future, in short, the legitimate object of prophecy."[92] If nature, gradually affirming life and shaken but ultimately benefited by the rain's buffeting, can attain its end, man, even midway in his life, can hope to realize his dream:

Aware only of my chimera
I noticed nothing round me 'till
one day the ripe spring surprised me
as its smiles began the field to fill.

Grey sprang the leaves
of swollen buds, bark and limb
and flowers, yellow, white and red
the scrap of land gayly trim.

The rain was golden arrow
and the sun on young fronds smiled;
on banks of deep river with sonorous roar
the poplars their own images beguiled.

After my life's long road, now for a first
time do I see springtime burst,
I spoke and then more stately did declame:

"How late comes this joy to me!"
and then, traveling on, as with wings there came
one more illusion fair—that I yet should see
my youth one future day come to be![93]

Ultimately it is human endeavor in the midst of the natural world which sustains hope, not the contemplation of one's own fancy. There is no evidence in man of such new life as spring displays: nascence in each particular of the landscape, variety of brightness, purity and richness in her colors, gilded youthfulness and transforming joy. Journeying has brought the poet this vision of genesis, of youth recaptured ("after my life's long road"). Thus, so long as he continues to journey ("then, traveling on . . ."), his dreams, renewed by the vision, may yet find fulfillment.

But youth would appear to be no more than a memory, a reality belonging essentially to the past. The life which spring restores to nature, however, is precisely that youth which she formerly possessed. Fields and trees which yesterday held beauty and today are bare, will, as the year progresses, return once again to the beginning of the cycle:

Love's poplar that yesterday held
nightingales upon your branch,
poplars that will tomorrow be
played as lyres by the spring wind.[94]

Poplars, the familiar trees of the Duero Valley, and indeed all trees, in which Machado observes this cycle, become for him an affirmation of renaissance. Through them the poet confronts temporality:

> In your old tree a young song you wear,
> the melody that yesterday's nightingale would claim.
> Poet, who wrinkles on your brow declare,
> your muse is noblest. Now Still is her name.
>
> Poet, nought but the soul is anchor to cling
> to shore, sharp spike and diamond shield
> and in December cold, rose garden as of spring,
> sun of the traveler, shadow for the road to yield.
>
> Poet, who wrinkles on your brow awake,
> your noble verse each day more youthful be
> that in the ancient tree a young song break,
> the eternal nightingale's new melody.[95]

Metaphorically uniting past ("yesterday's nightingale") to present, and thence to the possibility of future ("the eternal nightingale's new melody"), the old tree is the physical counterpart of the poet's muse. Both are essentially enduring: the tree, equally as the muse, is called "Now Still." The song of a former time has been preserved only because it is continued in this image. Memories are the poet's only weapon against time and his only inspiration to hope. So long as the present speaks with accents of the past, man possesses within himself the possibilities of permanence ("nought but the soul is anchor to cling / to shore"). His memories serve as a defense against temporality, a vision of a future life, a guide for life's journey, and a lingering shadow of presences to shelter and console him; though he be old and drawn toward the end of life, he harbors the possibility of new beginnings ("your noble verse each day more youthful be"). To speak of anything as eternal is to build a castle in the air unless the image is bound to something tangible and familiar which has already demonstrated a certain permanence. In this way, yesterday enduring in the nightingale in the old tree creates the hope of an imperishable tomorrow. The poet's voice communicates his individual spirit, which Unamuno has defined as "the effort of our recollection to endure, to make itself hope, the effort of our past to become future."[96]

This transformation of the past—here represented in metaphors from nature—is essentially an act of will, an active transition, which Machado expresses through a metaphor also drawn from nature, the labor of bees:

> In these endless
> galleries of memory
> where poor souls
> hang mementos sad,
>
> some festive costume
> moth-tattered now and worn,
> there the poet sees
> the work eternal
> of the golden bees
> which populate his dream.
>
> Poets, with your souls
> attuned to heaven high
> whether in battle cruel
> or in tranquil garden set,
>
> the new honey here we make
> from sorrows old,
> the gown white and pure
> patiently we sew
> and 'neath the sun we forge
> a new shield of war.[97]

Volition, however, produces a desire for and a dream of transformed reality, not reality itself. Just as eternity is a possibility and a wish, not a fact, the past renewed is the offspring of a dream ("the golden bees / which populate his dream"). Yet a creative dream is desirable: its inhabitants are golden and their labor eternal, as elsewhere the dream itself is called a blessed illusion.[98] There too, golden bees are described as making sweet honey from old bitterness. What is old and pertinent to the past becomes new, the beginning of existence; what is sorrowful and bitter becomes sweet and desirable; and the innocence of life without the imprint of time is restored.

The bees, of course, go on making honey quite independent of dreams, a honey real and substantial. Man, on the contrary, creates only illusions since his efforts begin and end in uncertainty. Thus, the image of the bees is not only a metaphor indicating the power to transform, but also part of the creative cycle of nature which both parallels and contrasts with human endeavor:

Man in thought,
how far seems the buzz
of bees and the work they wrought!

For the fair world, a
shadow veil you toss, and go
thinking you see what the compass-
hands in shadow show.
While the bee labors, fleet
and makes sweet
with the flavor of field and sun,
I truth go scattering
that falsehood is, the sputtering
dregs of my crucible or bowl.
From the sea to perception bent,
and then unto conception go,

from concept the idea to pursue
—oh, what a lovely task to do!—
from idea one advances to the sea.
And will again at the beginning be.[99]

Although both the poet and the bee are performing an action —the former cerebral, the latter physical—the reality of nature is far removed from human speculation ("how far seems the buzz / of bees and the work they wrought"). Both functions are creative, but the human, as described in the second stanza, is veiled by a subjective interpretation, a shadow over the real world. Being a shadow, this subjectivity has no substance, except when, in contrast with physical objects, it acquires a visible surface dimension. This, being perceivable and measurable, creates the illusion of reality. Upon the basis of this illusion, this faulty understanding, the poet builds his philosophy. Thus his action, like that of the bees, is creative, but while the bee produces a tangible good from an actual element of nature, the poet's good is a deception ("truth . . . that falsehood is") obscured and perceived by him alone. Despite its short-comings, this human effort nevertheless gives continuity to experience and meaning to the unknown through the known. The basis of all understanding is sense knowledge ("perception"), from which we form concepts of the nature of particular objects and experiences. These constitute our contact with absolutes ("ideas"), which, inasmuch as they are abstractions and our intellect fully comprehends only sensory things, remain essentially unknown. But the achievement of limited understanding, even confused understanding, and the dedication to the quest sustain man in a continuing search.

Various aspects of water, roads, and the day's cycle have been shown to suggest—as well as images of new flowers, foliage restored to trees, and the honey making of bees—both the transformation of the past and the subjective character of human hope and understanding. Spring, however, is the essential image of life renewed since it immediately indicates a renaissance and communicates this spirit to more particular images: "April contains a thousand rains"[100]; "Beyond the green plain, on the flowered crest / perhaps the end of your road is near"[101]; "A spring dawn said to me: I flower in your shadowed heart."[102] The season slowly brings the long desired beauty to semiarid Soria, the land of Machado's most intense personal associations. Thus it embodies his thoughts of Leonor, memories, hopes and moments of confidence: "sometimes I firmly believe I shall be reunited with her."[103]

During the year between his return from Paris with his seriously ill wife, September 1911, and her death in August 1912, Machado did not return to teaching but rather dedicated his time to Leonor's care, and wrote only one poem, a vision of spring in the midst of death:

> On the elm old, split by lightning ray
> and all its center now a rotten core,
> with April rains and sun of May
> a few green leaves appear once more.
>
> Oh, ageless elm of grey hills dark
> above the Duero's bank. A yellow mould
> stains your whitewashed even bark
> and gnaws your dusty trunk grown old.
>
> You will not be, as here the bank along
> the poplars guard the river and the road,
> a home to nightingale's soft song.
>
> An army of ants gnaw and their nests load
> and their destruction sow. Its guts within,
> silent, their grey nets, the spiders spin.

Before they hew you down, elm of Duero's shore
with woodman's ax and e'er they bore
your grain and bell ropes make
and oxen yoke and planks of cart,
before you see the fire take
your life in some small house apart
along the road, tomorrow
before the wind uproot and harrow
you or mountain gust should rack
you, e'er the river drives you to the sea
through crevices and valley crack,
I, elm, would describe as I go
your gracious branch in green leaf-net.
My heart does also hope to know,
which unto light and life is set,
another miracle that spring may sow.[104]

The poet does not deny the proximity of death; rather he affirms and even dwells upon it. The reality of spring ("April rains and sun of May") does not contradict that of death, but rather transcends it, not revitalizing the entire tree, nor saving it from destruction, but leaving some little evidence of life. The entire poem is an acknowledgment of the elm's fate: it beauty rotted, its vitality and joy transformed into grey corruption, and the song of birds which dwelt in its branches changed into the silent, corrosive labor of ants and spiders. Above all, it must cease to be a part of nature and must, therefore, lose its identity. The preposition "before" affirms the inevitable. But, as he acknowledges death, the poet seeks to preserve for himself the reality of life. Without the visible miracle of a few green leaves, he cannot even venture to imagine such a miracle in the human world ("*another* miracle"). Viewing this frail resurgence, however, he dares hope—a hope born of love, not of reason ("my heart does also hope to know . . .")—that for man too there is a truth like the sun of May and a source of regeneration like the

April rains ("my heart . . . which unto light and life is set") which will restore to him the life desired.

Since he seeks life renewed rather than life preserved, the poet's hope is not extinguished by Leonor's death. Each spring bears new witness to the cyclical fulfillment of the desire for rebirth and thus vanquishes the fear of death's finality and of the unknown:

> As the snow melts, the mountains
> stand out from the range.
> The meadow grows green
> with April sun, the valley
> is a green flame and bears
> life, effortlessly.
> The soul contemplates a butterfly
> —atlas of the world—and dreams.
> With the plum trees in blossom and the field
> a glaucous vapor beyond the shore
> about the branches,
> and the first brambles shooting forth white buds,
> with this sweet breeze
> that conquers death and stone
> flows forth the bitterness which stifles me
> awaiting Her . . .[105*]

From the distant mountains becoming ever more immediate and from the impression of nature as a whole, the description progresses through particular concepts and scenes to a specific image, concurrently developing the affirmation of life. In spring, Machado is not concerned with the remote but with the proximate; not with the whole but with the particular and personal ("The bitterness which stifles me"); and with this new life not as a principle of growth or a source of beauty but as that which

* Death: Feminine in Spanish, death is frequently identified by the feminine pronoun capitalized.

triumphs over death. At first spring only delineates and colors the landscape. Almost at once, however, the color connotes vitality ("the valley / is a green flame") and the spiritual character of the season. Hence it stirs the poetic imagination and occasions dreams ("The soul contemplates a butterfly—atlas of the world—and dreams."). But death is more real than a dream. Thus the poet seeks an equally real and individual evidence of rebirth, turning to the images of trees and bramble bushes. In the midst of nature flowering, life transcends both death and time, implicitly suggested in the unchanging stone which, contrasting with mutable things, communicates to man a temporal consciousness. And since his anguish is not a reaction against death itself, but against its finality, the vision of regeneration in spring makes it possible for him to acknowledge and await death without despair.

It is precisely his certainty of this yearly rebirth that imparts reality to Machado's personal hopes:

> Palacio, dear friend,
> does spring now
> adorn the limbs of poplars
> along the river bank and road? To the uplands
> of the Duero spring comes late
> but how lovely is she when she comes!
> Have the old elms
> new leaves now?
> The azaleas will be naked still
> And snow will cover yet the sierra crest.
> On massive Moncayo white and rose
> soon beautiful against the sky of Aragón
> are there brambles flowering
> among the rocks dark grey
> and marguerites pure white
> and amid the tiny herbs?

Atop bell towers will
the storks soon arrive.
The wheat fields will be green
and dusty mules will tread the land
and farmers go out sowing their late seed
with April rains. The bees will
draw from thyme and from rosemary.
And are the plum trees now in bloom? Do violets
remain? Some furtive hunter, partridge
decoy beneath long cape,
is surely to be seen. Palacio, my friend,
are there yet nightingales along the banks?
With the first lilies
and the first roses in the vale,
of a clear afternoon, ascend unto Espino's peak,
to the high land where now lies her home.[106]

The physical world alone is certain and, therefore, explicitly described; the poem's human circumstances are only implied. Even the immediate countryside is incidental to the countryside of the poet's memories. Of no concern to him are his actual surroundings except as an indication of his absence from the land remembered and as a contrast with and affirmation of the eventual coming of late Sorian spring. Being a relative term, "late" implies that it is already spring somewhere else. Similarly, the reason for his inquiry is obliquely suggested in the opening line, since the poet is addressing Leonor's cousin, and equally indirectly in the closing line which identifies the Duero tableland, flanked by mountains, as her land.

Soria is, for Machado, Leonor's land: "Five years in the countryside of Soria, sacred to me now—there I married; there I lost my wife, whom I adored."[107] The Espino is, more specifically, the place of Leonor's grave, a land made doubly hers by her abiding in it. Throughout the poem he strives to evoke her as part of reality: in a growing awareness not of irrevocable death but rather of life and transformation in nature; in his own increasing uncertainty and in images which foreshadow the final verses. As the landscape becomes progressively inhabited and active, suggestions of rebirth multiply: new leaves upon the trees, flowers among the rocks, etc. At the same time there occurs a transition from uncertainty to actuality. To his initial question the poet responds with an acknowledgment of winter ("The azaleas will be naked still / and snow will cover yet the sierra crest."). But because of the changes which he remembers from former springs, he becomes more confident ("atop bell towers will / the storks soon arrive;" "The wheat fields will be green;" "farmers . . . sowing their late seed;" etc.). And if these signs of spring are present, all the season's promises of beauty, lyricism and rebirth are about to be fulfilled. In their fulfillment is his most intimate desire realized. The poem's images echo in the final scene of nature transformed: Moncayo in its neighboring peak, Espino; the white berry blossoms and daisies among the iris; trees and flowers in the rose garden; and the total impression of activity in the image of real, physical movement: "ascend unto Espino's peak." The entire poem has communicated reality, certainty and life to his hope.

Nevertheless, this reality remains his own creation. The absent beloved is present only as an illusion. Thus he can hear her voice only in a dream "as a new bell, / a virginal bell / of a springtime dawn. / Your voice and touch / were in my dreams so real."[108] In the physical world even spring is transient. The enduring spring to which he aspires must be, therefore, a vision evoked through a dream:

> It matters not that golden wine
> should lie within your crystal cup
> or bitter gall the clear glass deface.

You know the secret galleries
of the soul, the dream roads
and the tranquil afternoon wherein
must perish these.—There await you

life's silent spirits all
who to a garden of eternal spring
you will one day with them bear.[109]

From the substance of life, joy and sadness ("golden wine" and "bitter gall"), whose balance and alternation give to man his sense of time, memories arise, and from these, dreams which overcome the limitation of life itself. Although life tends inevitably to death, there is no sense of despair, since in that final moment the poet is met by the spirits of prophecy. They presage rebirth not death; they are guides to a new life which is eternal. And yet because they wait at the end of a dream journey, the poem concludes on a note of uncertainty, of a future vague but intimately united to the image of permanence.

In order to realize fully the desires expressed through images of the spring it is necessary that the season's life be eternal. The beauty of nature is not an end in itself. The landscape in autumn may suggest loveliness, but it stands doomed on the threshold of death. Moreover, a barren autumnal landscape suggests not only decline but an inheritance of misery, spiritual as well as physical. The poet must return to memory and to illusions of eternity. Spring is the shape of things restored. But the desire to realize an eternal spring is a dream; the nature of human reason prohibits a certain vision of that which lies beyond death and dreams.

The Dialogue with Time

THE RECOGNITION that human understanding has definite limitations does not prevent a constant inquiry into the essence of life and a continuing search for truth. This juxtaposition of uncertainty, desire and search has appeared in every image the poet uses to represent man's temporal condition. Because the conflict between his consciousness and his dreams—"I live," writes Machado, "in peace with other men and at war with myself."[1]—forces him to seek reconciliation in a reality independent of his own being, the poet is engaged in a dialogue throughout his life.

In every facet of life to which he addresses himself he faces the same enigma, the same barriers to understanding. As he penetrates the apparent reality of memories, images of a familiar landscape, and the temporal conditions of man and his surroundings, they retreat into mystery and shadow. In "Los sueños dialogados" (The Dream Dialogues) Machado confronts the entire landscape of nature and human experience, encompassing in the scope of the poem the recollections, perceptions, hopes and fears which he has encountered singly and in various associations of images: water, roads and cycles of life.

Always, upon addressing an object, he has been forced to conclude that the object is no more than his own interpretation projected. In his dialogue with time, particular images are veils to be swept aside so that, ultimately, the poet directly addresses the unknown.

I

Amid the high plains memory yields
to me your face! . . . My words evoke
the meadow green, the arid fields
and brambles amid rocks as ashen-grey as smoke.

Black oaks that bow to memory's will
appear upon the hills, as poplars line
the river bank, shepherds scale a hill,
one city window glows and it is mine,

nay, ours. Now do you see? Beyond
toward Aragón, Moncayo's white-rose peak will knife
the sky. And burning clouds as one red pond,

and single star will light the blue, my wife.
Across the Duero, Santana's massive mound
grows purple in the day's spent, silent life.

II

Why, you say, flees toward higher empty plain
my heart, that on this fertile shore was placed,
and though in land of farm and mariner I might remain,
sighs my spirit for the lone Castilian waste?

No man may choose his love. One day
my fate to grey cliffs bent me to arrive
where cold the falling snow masks with ice spray
those shadows which the dead black oaks inscribe.

Then from that barren scrap of Spain I carry
down to you, flowered margin of a southern river flowing
one solitary spring of bitterest rosemary.

My heart dwells where born, where growing
not in life, in love. On the Duero's bank I tarry.
A whitewashed wall and cemetery cypress' tall crest
blowing.

III

The glowing embers of the sunset, lady,
rent now the cloud that coming storm denotes,
have traced upon the rocks of far and shady
hill a glow resplendent that a dawn connotes.

But curdled dawn that's scratched in frozen stone
which to the traveler terror is and fright
more fierce than lion come upon one day alone
or giant bear encountered in the mountain's height.

Distraught with flames of love, that dreams enmesh,
that hopes envision and dark fears bespeak,
I journey toward the sea, unto forgetfulness

—not as the rocket that in night most bleak
about the planet turns in cycles numberless.
No, call me not, for I cannot a road returning seek.

IV

Oh loneliness, my sole companion, you
who, muse of prophecy, words on my voice once laid
that never had I thought to beg nor to pursue,
answer, telling me with whom my dialogue is made.

Far from the noisy masquerade, apart a space,
I here my sorrow entertain, companionless, alone
with you, my lady of the veiled face,
veiled always in conversations we have known.

And now I think: be I whoever I may be,
for mystery no more in this self lies
that in the mirror of the soul I see.

From your beloved voice alone does mystery arise.
Then show me now your face that fixed on me
I should, thus seeing, know your diamond eyes.[2]

From a specific physical landscape to complete abstraction; from the known and remembered world to enigma; from conversation with a recognized companion, his wife, to dialogue with the unknown; from self to the other—that other to which existence relates and which Jaspers calls Transcendence or the Encompassing—the four sonnets pass, illuminating particulars of the poet's life and thought as he inquires into the essence of reality. The ultimate question—"answer, telling me with whom my dialogue is made"—is the result of his Proustian consciousness of the past. Through an awareness of the mutability of all things and a purposeful effort to evoke former experiences, he realizes that in a dialogue with the objects of his perception he does not address reality but rather its representations, objects of his own creation.[3] He thus confronts the problem of objectivity only after having sought a subjective explanation of life ("be I whoever I may be / for mystery no more in this self lies / that in the mirror of the soul I see. / From your beloved voice alone does mystery arise.").

The first sonnet is a dialogue with an individual memory, with Leonor; the poet is confident that he knows with whom he speaks. His certainty is based upon the apparent reality of nature: the contrast of green meadow and flowers with the rocky arid plain which evokes Soria and the unaltered mountains. Less certain is Leonor's presence; the recollection is momentarily interrupted as the poet seeks a confirmation for his vision: "do you see?" he asks her. Although the landscape remains, time gradually obscures the scene, and in the dying day ("in the day's spent, silent life") no one answers him.

Hence the poet turns from the landscape of memory to the immediate, visible countryside ("Then from that scrap of Spain, I carry / down to you, flowered margin of a southern river flowing . . ."). Love, not wisdom, determines his vision, as snow veils the dead trees. His understanding of Soria is subjective; his penetration of the past, an emotional response ("My heart dwells where born, where growing / not in life, in love."); his only tangible possession, witness to his bitter loneliness, a bit of Castilian rosemary.

The obvious contrast between the barren landscape remembered and the animate present does not, however, confer either permanance or objectivity on the world now perceived. That which exists and which we call real is, in the metaphysics of Juan de Mairena, identical with the apparent, because it is subject to change: "reality is an infinite apparentness, a constant and inexhaustible possibility of appearance."[4] Fleeting time dominates the third sonnet, so that the poet is again drawn from the physical world into uncertainty, and from visible images into a fearful vision. Once hopefully suggestive of the future, the light of dawn is now deformed by the terror which man feels upon contemplating his journey's end ("But curdled dawn that's scratched in frozen stone . . ."). Because he finds himself in the midst of uncertainty, he can no longer clearly identify his partner in dialogue. To wake from his dream and to cease to journey is to die, to lose even the tenuous contact with the remembered exprience of life ("I journey toward the sea, unto forgetfulness"); with both fear and hope he approaches the invitable moment ("I cannot a road returning seek").

Death is the essentially subjective experience, the totally personal moment which no man can share with or reveal to another. Endowed with a vision of life's totality and conscious of his own finitude, with whom shall the poet converse if not with the mystery inherent in that vision ("with you, my lady of the veiled face"). The quest for a reality outside himself, a realm free of subjective interpretations, which was born in a particular situation of life—the life with Leonor—becomes the recognition that self-knowledge will never reveal to him the other whom he seeks.

Machado as philosopher is not, of course, a commentary on Machado as poet. Yet Juan de Mairena and Abel Martín are participants in the poet's vision. Just as being, for the poet, is identical with the search for an existence independent of himself, for them philosophy is a mode of apprehending an absolute reality: "the monad . . . which would not be a mirror or a representation of the universe, but the universe itself as conscious activity: the great eye which sees all in seeing itself."[5] Pursuing truth the poet also desires to see the mystery which comprehends him ("your diamond eyes"), for to see is to understand.

Poetry as a dialogue of man with time is a voice addressing human limitations in images: a river doomed to disappear into the sea, a road created as one journeys, the shadows which haunt life, the love reborn only in dreams. Since time steals everything from man, man has only himself with whom to speak ("Oh loneliness, my sole companion"). But he desires to converse with eternity: "man is the only animal who wishes to be saved."[6] The insistence with which he confronts the unknown, asking, imploring, demanding to know, is born of this desire.

Spain: The National Aspect of Temporality

THE QUEST for truth, the desire to know, and the problem of time concern not only Machado but, as we have remarked, his contemporaries as well. They involve not only individual problems, but also the fate of Spain. In describing his own attitudes, Baroja, never willing to acknowledge the existence of a Generation of 1898, in effect defines the Generation's concept of patriotism:

I am normally preoccupied with desiring what is best for my country, but I reject the patriotism of lies. I wish that Spain were the greatest country in the world. . . . But next to this patriotism of desire must exist reality . . . for patriotism is national truth enflamed by a desire for the nation's wellbeing and by sympathy.[1]

Thus he also characterizes Machado's patriotism. Even as he deplores the shortcomings of contemporary society, he believes that his country, once rich in achievement, still possesses the capacity for greatness. Both her strength and her decay he finds reflected in the countryside of Castile: austere grandeur and firmness, the rocky landscape and its grey, arid plains dotted with crumbling ruins which evoke spiritual sterility.

The adjectives which Machado repeatedly applies to Castile and to particular features of the land—arid, harsh, grey, dry, hard, cold, etc.—can, depending upon the context of a specific poem, suggest the virtues as well as the defects of the country. There is no algebraic formula, such as Manuel García Viño suggests,[2] whereby adjectival and adverbial modification produces a single tone—dusty grey—and a single mood throughout Machado's poetry. Isolating the modifiers which he most frequently uses only serves to verify that they do not have any absolute significance and that they cannot be considered apart from specific images.

In a similar manner the connotation derived from images of water and roads, from the cycles of day and year, function within Machado's total vision of Spain but never become separable symbols. Especially as applied to interpretations of national character, the roads over the harsh landscape are at once symbolic journeys and Castile's lime-powdered highways; the rivers that rush to the sea are both doomed life and real rivers, the Duero and the Guadalquivir, images in two worlds and the union of both.

In Machado's poems, description, imagery, and elaboration are always secondary to the total vision. Poetry which glories in elaboration for its own sake and which subjugates the object to its description receives from Juan de Mairena a scathing condemnation:

> The same shortsightedness of intuition which, incapable of attaining to ideas, leads to conceptualism* and thence to pure verbal ingenuity, breeds the culturalist metaphor, the dry and arid topology of Góngora, the arduous disordering of generic images, at root nothing but definitions, subject to the exercises of mere logic, that only an inept criticism or a depraved taste could confuse with poetry.[3]

* Conceptualism and culturalism are specific forms of baroque literature in Spain.

In singularly baroque fashion, Machado thus dismisses the baroque poets.

But if the dismissal itself is a conceptual tour de force, Machado's poetry is never this. The austerity of his verse is the austerity of the reflected landscape. For the Castilian meseta and also Soria are rocky, grey and arid. Repeated references to these qualities, together with familiar images of the countryside—herbs, flowering brambles, rows of poplars, oak trees, grazing sheep and bulls, the Duero and the peaks of the Guadarrama—serve primarily to evoke the country and only secondarily to characterize it spiritually.

The Generation of 1898 has, in Laín-Entralgo's words, both discovered and invented the Castilian landscape.[4] They discovered it by perceiving and communicating a vision of beauty in its severity and bold lines; they invented it by tracing parallels between its physical properties and the Spanish soul. Frequently introduced by Machado, for example, is the evergreen oak *(encina)*, common to rural Castile: in summer less majestic than the broad foliage of the mountain oak *(roble)* and less graceful than the poplars; and, in winter, its leaves dead and its flowers gone, displaying only somber, darkest green. Yet in this tree Machado perceives the fortitude and humility he interprets as typically Castilian:

> Always steadfast, never changed,
> impassive, venerable and true,
> in serenity and sturdy, you
> eternal black oak range
>
> . . . . . .
>
> and you the oak grove of Madrid
>
> . . . . . .
>
> with your native austerity
> an answer make
> to all that's vain, false or fake
> and to polite urbanity.[5]

Similarly the familiar merino flocks and pasturing bulls suggest the dual character of Soria: mystical and warlike.[6] However, sheep, so essential to the Castilian peasant livelihood, may also indicate the country's poverty, as in the image "where the squalid merino graze."[7] Both the oak grove and the squalid merino can be cited to illustrate the variations Machado introduces into imagery. Grazing sheep primarily indicate life, as in the poem "Pascuas de Resurección" (Easter)[8] but the reference to an emaciated sheep, together with other impressions of poverty, prepare for Machado's characterization of the Sorian spring as a humble springtime.[9]

As the essentially idyllic image of sheep can be used to express poverty, so negative adjectives can acquire an affirmative connotation. *Adusto* (noun: *adustez*) may be translated as hot, scorching, grim, sullen, or stern. Yet the poet can say, praising Spain, "con tu adustez castellana," because he gives to sternness the connotation of nobility, opposing this to vanity and pomp.[10]

Clearly then the poet owes much in his national poems both to the physical appearance of Castile and to his use of qualities traditionally associated with the native Castilian. In this sense his choice of images is somewhat more predictable than in his more personal poems. Both, however, owe their archetypes to the processes of the land and the basic images to the Castilian landscape.

Both the archetypes and the basic images are time oriented. For what can be said of the essence of Spain can be said also of past centuries. The oak groves, the world of the medieval poet Berceo, with his "lines like furrows in the arid fields with the blue mountains afar,"[11] the unaltered life of the shepherd and farmer —all provide bonds between the past and the present. Scenes from and reflections upon past centuries originate in nature. A portrait of Soria in the changing seasons or contemplated from a hillside on a summer afternoon becomes a vision of former greatness fallen into decay. And the women of the Mancha suggest, first, thoughts of their ancestors, historical and literary and, finally, of Dulcinea who, as an illusion, inspired the noble ideals of don Quijote.

The emphasis which Machado places upon constant elements in the national character, his lament for the present and his ideals for a new Spain, reflect his rapport with other members of the Generation. At the same time these present, in the national context, the concern with single details from the past which characterizes his memories of a Sevillan childhood or his years with Leonor in Soria. Both are compositions based on a few remembered images. They become the poetic equivalent of Unamuno's intra-history, which the philosopher sees "beneath the history of fleeting events . . . that other profound history of permanent facts, a silent history, that of the poor farmers who day after day without rest rise before the sun to till their fields."[12]

Machado does not, however, echo another man's ideas. His similarity with Unamuno is less important than the sources of his own conclusions. Five years as a schoolteacher in Soria taught him not only love for that countryside but an awareness of the vices of his countrymen:

> The evil man abounds in field and town,
> one capable of insane vice and crimes depraved,
> who an ugly soul hides beneath his peasant gown,
> and who is to the seven deadly sins enslaved.[13]

Yet he also senses a capacity for nobility and accomplishment in these people,[14] from which are born his hope for a vital future and his challenge to a new generation.

Finally, in noting the attitudes underlying Machado's national themes, one cannot ignore his fervent and permanent republicanism. Although a speculative philosopher, Machado is never a speculative political theorist; his loyalty to the Republic is a personal, even an emotional, response to an idea. According to his own description this ideal was born in his youth:

When I was a child there was a republican emotion abroad in Spain. I remember having wept with enthusiasm hearing the Marseillaise during a victorious reception for Salmerón on his return from Barcelona. Everyone spoke of republican ideas and these ideas were at least a sincere emotion, a noble one to my way of thinking. Why, then, slay it?[15]

He continued to ask "Why slay it?" even when admitting that the Second Republic, as a reality, was not all he had desired.[16] When the staunchest supporters and, indeed, many of those responsible for the Republican constitution decided that the actual government was a cause hardly worth supporting with their lives, and that the war was a battle all but lost, the mass exodus from Spain began. Machado, however, chose to remain, first in Valencia, writing for *Hora de España*, and then retreating to Barcelona and fleeing to France only as that city was about to fall.[17]

One does not ask that poems be political manifestos. Machado often leaves his political comments to Mairena, although attacks on the nation find their way into several poems. But their presence is an emotional rather than an intellectual response, similar to the emotional response to Soria, qualified by his love and his personal recollections of Seville.

It is also a personal response which characterizes his descriptions of most national institutions. Descriptions such as

> Spain of brass bands and tambourines
> closed and churchy and very
> devoted to the bull ring and to Mary
> . . . . which prays and spits
> when the situation calls for the use of wits,[18]

which distress some of his critics—Serrano Poncela and Laín Entralgo are determined to prove that this is both an exaggeration and not poetry[19]—are neither analyses nor attacks but reactions to the customs of the country as Machado has observed them.

The harshnes of the images is consistent with the extent of his disgust and no more negative than the surrealistic scenes of "Otro clima."[20] The frequent reference to Spain or a Spaniard yawning graphically and immediately identifies apathy, lack of idealism and abuse of the intellect.

In his treatment of Spain, as in his more personal poems, Machado endeavors to represent temporal totality: past glories, dissatisfaction with the present and desire for a better Spain, envisioned through past achievements and contrasted to present decay. As he articulates his own uncertainties through images of shadow, so he sees evil as a physical shadow on the land—the shadow of Cain—bearing testimony to decadence but also challenging the present to redeem itself. Ruins also bear testimony both to former greatness and to present squalor:

Soria, cold land, *Soria pure,*
at the head of Extramadure,
with your warrior's fort array
above the Duero, in ruins, decay,
with your rotted tumbling walls,
and your time-despoiled halls.

Cities dead of nobles proud,
soldiers and of huntsmen's crowd,
of doors emblem-emblazoned each
a hundred age's blood most blue,
of greyhounds, lean and starving too,
thin and sharp hounds which reach,
swarm and prowl
down sordid alleyways and cluttered row
and at the midnight hour howl
when sounds the cawing of the crow.

Soria, cold land, now the bell
in tower strikes: one: And there
stands Soria of Castile's wasted spell
beneath the moon: how fine and fair.[22]

Ancient houses, each emblazoned with its coat of arms, suggest the futility of noble lineage, since the sights and sounds which now dominate the city present an impression of wretchedness. And yet, perceiving the city outlined in moonlight, its decay hidden, the poet, even as he hears the howling dogs, senses an intransient beauty. The Audiencia clock has sounded the hour, century after century, towering over the changing city, like the spirit of Soria which the poet loves, uncorrupted by the physical rot, the hunger and the misery which haunt its streets.

Just as sordidness is the city's physical inheritance, emptiness is bequeathed to man by an idle past:

This man is neither of yesterday nor of a future day,
but is of never; incarnation is of Spain's decay,
and fruit neither ripe nor rotten he,
but a fruit to throw away,
from that Spain that's past and never come to be,
that Spain whose head is white with age today.[23]

Spain's tragedy, as Machado interprets it, is epitomized in the provincial native, who lives neither for obligations of tradition nor dreams of progress. It is not a despoiled ideal which he laments, but the utter lack of any ideal, the futility of time passing uselessly ("that Spain that's past and never come to be, / that Spain whose head is white with age today").

Machado envisions both temporal contrast and comparison as synthesizing the complex relationship of Spain's history, her national character and her present state, both physical and spiritual:

It was a day in mid-July. A fine and pleasant day,
that I, alone, through fissures of the rock made my way,
seeking shadowed ledges, slowly bent upon the path.
I stopped to wipe my brow, moist with the sun's wrath
and to catch my breath when to breathing hard I fell,
and, again, my body forward bent, climbing well,
while in my right hand, as to sustain my pace,
supported by a cane, like some member of a pastoral race,
I scaled the high hill where are wont to rest
rapacious high-flown birds that feed upon and nest
amid the mountain's strong scented herbs—rosemary, sage,
lavender and thyme. On bitter fields the sun vents its rage.

A wide-winged vulture in arched majestic flight
crossed, a solitary traveler in the sky's blue light.
And I could afar devise a mountain sharply rising out
the curved hills, seeming a shield or a redoubt,
and red-washed foothills all about this land's uncolored shore
—some tattered rags of harness lay, remnants of forgotten war—
the barren heights where twists the Duero in its row
to arc about the land as might the archer's bow
describe itself before the plain. Soria is a fortress for
Castile's tower before neighbor Aragón's warlike door.
I saw enclosed by hills that toward the distance spread from me,
dark with black oaks, crowned by Castile's native tree;
the rocks stood naked above a few parched humble fields
where Merinos pastured and the great black bull kneels
to chew the herbs, while there along the river's banks
the green poplars to sun and clear air show their ranks,
as, silently, across the distant plains, some travelers appear
—how small they seem!—carts, horsemen and muleteer—,
and cross the bridge with ancient stone arcade above;
shadowed by the bridge's bay, run the silvered waters of
the Duero.

The Duero moves across the heart of oak
that in Iberia and Castile lies.

Land that sorrow and nobility bespoke,

land of high fields, rocks and cliffs that naked wait the breeze,
untilled its crops, devoid of water way or stand of trees,
decrepit cities dot its face, no inn relieves its way,
but rustics stand agape, inept for dance or song and stray
afar as rivers do they flee the dying home,
rushing as your water to the sea, Castile, so they roam,

Miserable Castile, who yesterday did reign,
wrapped now in rags, what you know not you disdain.
Do you hope or sleep or dream? Or blood once shed recall
when fired with zeal you harkened to the swift sword's call?
All things must change, flow on, journey, flee or cycle make;
the sea and hill are changed and eye that of their vision does
partake.
Gone? Above the field hovers still the ghost
of a land that in God's name armed a warrior host.

Mother in that distant time of captains brave
can scarcely claim as stepchild street urchin or slave,
Castile is not she who once in generosity could know no peer
when don Rodrigo de Vivar returned in pomp most dear,
in pride of fortune newly gained and opulence to bring
and give the gardens of Valencia unto Alfonse his king,
nor she who, as befitting to her name,
her court besought that they in conquest claim
the Indian rivers wide; mother then of soldier bold,
of warrior and chieftain who returned laden down by gold
and silver bound for Spain, in galleons regal rode,
of men as falcons for the prey and for the fight as lions showed.
Philosophers on convent soup now nourished and sustained
upon the endless firmament their contemplation trained,
impassive if in dreams, as from afar,
to noises of Levante's merchants on the docks, are
not aware nor question make and so
now open the portals of her house the war does throw.

Miserable Castile, who yesterday did reign,
wrapped now in rags, what you know not you disdain.

The sun begins to set. Far in the distant city ring
the bells whose harmonies the night winds bring
—the black-shawled women rosary beads to tell now go—.
From somewhere in the rocks dart two fair weasels, though
on seeing me they swift withdraw, and then peer out again
—how curious they seem!—Dark grows the plain.
Upon the white road one open inn I see alone,
open to the shadowed field as to deserted cliffs of stone.[24]

The landscape of Castile provides a link between Spain's past and her present and thus affords the poet not only a view of his surroundings, but also an insight into the essence of his country. Thus in contrasting yesterday and today—"Miserable Castile, who yesterday did reign, / wrapped now in rags what you know not you disdain."—he understands what is constant in the Castilian character.

Menéndez Pidal, in his analysis "Los españoles en su historia," observes that the proud, unbending national spirit, responsible for so many of Spain's greatest achievements, has also bred its most serious defects, particularly extremism, exaggerated devotion to tradition, peninsular isolation, and an inability to compromise.[25] What for the historian is a conclusion drawn from study, is for the poet an intuitive understanding, equally exact and equally valid. But Machado is also a student, not of documents and texts, but of history reflected in literature and celebrated by the people—of which don Rodrigo de Vivar, the Cid, is the preeminent example—and of the countryside. Hence his vision is also a conclusion, first from the scene before him and then from the past which it evokes.

The conception of Spain as a spiritual whole originates, as do all valid abstractions, in a particular and concrete image, identified and described through its details. The first and final stanzas constitute both the frame in which the poet's observations are set up and a touchstone for their reality. Life continues and time passes as the poet meditates, so that the hill which he ascended during the day, he descends as night is falling. This short span of hours bears witness to the constant temporality of all life which Machado acknowledges in his meditation: "All things must change, flow on, journey, flee or cycle make / the sea and hill are changed and eye that of their vision does partake."

From his vantage point, the poet, attracted by the flight of a vulture, gazes out upon the entire landscape. He commands a view of the rocky, barren face of the land with but a trace of meadow; of the perennial sheep and bull; of a few travelers who, with their age-old means of conveyance, could belong to any century; of an old bridge and the older river. Thus he views those things in the world which are relatively unchanged, constants about which he can make absolute statements: "The Duero moves across the heart of oak / that in Iberia and Castile lies." But evidence of change is also present: "some tattered rags of harness lay, remnants of forgotten war," physical testimony to decay and ruin.

Machado's is not, however, a disinterested eye: the visible scene elicits a personal and emotional response directed toward the land itself, bare and unproductive; toward the crumbling cities and deserted roads; and toward the people, without purpose and without joy, fleeing the arid land. With an awareness of the unchanged landscape, of decay and of the unhappy present, the poet paints the soul of Spain: "Miserable Castile . . ."

His lament for his country is more than an awareness of the present. It implies the idealism and dedication responsible for former achievements ("Or blood once shed recall / when fired with zeal you harkened to the swift sword's call?"); the inevitable change to which all things are subject; and the memory which preserves a dream of ideals and greatness ("Gone? Above the field hovers still the ghost / of a land that in God's name armed a warrior host."). Although nature, even in its most stable elements, is mutable, this is not an altogether aimless movement, since some change, as the physical world reveals, is cyclic.

But Spain's history reveals only destruction and decline. Once victor and *conquistadora,* Castile is now a victim, the last of her great empire swept away. But the pride of the Cid, no longer justified by accomplishments, and disdain still linger in the sad Castile of the present: "wrapped now in rags, what you know not you disdain." Machado's description is a reflection of the past as well as of the contemporary scene. His thoughts lead him back to the present: "and so / now open the portals of her house the war does throw,"* repeating, like a refrain, "Miserable Castile . . ."; and back to the landscape where "some tattered scraps *(harapos)* of harness lay," echoing spiritual raggedness: "wrapped now in rags" *(harapos)*.

Attentive once more to his surroundings, Machado is aware of the passage of time, of those things in human life which repeat themselves almost unaltered—the old women in black go to their evening prayers as they have gone for generations—and of spirited, playful life in nature: "From somewhere in the rocks dart two fair weasels though / on seeing me they swift withdraw, and then peer out again / —how curious they seem!"

All movement in the countryside has been slow and stately: the poet's ascent through the rocky hillside, the vulture's flight, the distant and silent travelers, the Duero. The land itself has been portrayed as stark and lonely. But in this epilogue to the poet's thoughts there appear two frisky animals. And although they are weasels, typically nocturnal and hardly the most endearing of creatures, the poet, seeing them scurry about and peer out

* The war to which the poet refers is the Spanish American War.

at him, calls them *fair* weasels. Here he also observes, in the midst of the rocky, barren land, a single inn, an exception to the portrait of ruin and total abandonment which he himself has painted.

Vital impressions are nevertheless marginal to the theme of Castile in her rags. The Spanish peasant dwells in these lands upon which the shadow of Cain falls, where this specter even hovers over the schoolchildren in a portrait on the classroom wall: "In a poster / the figure of Cain / in flight and Abel dead."[26] From this awareness of festering evil in the soul of his countrymen arises Machado's only narrative poem, "La tierra de Alvargonzález,"[27] in the original prose version a tale of fratricide, while in the ballad a portrait of one murder, the slaying of Alvargonzález by his sons, Juan and Martín. In both versions the image of Cain appears, representing envy and all the vices which it engenders:

> The blood of Cain flows
> in the country laborer's veins.
>
> . . . . . .
>
> And greed for land to own
> sees inheritance in every grave.

Nothing of benefit either to themselves or to their nation can be expected from the labor of men corrupted by their own base passions and vile acts, as, symbolically, the soil which Martín and Juan till bears no fruit. Their bloody act literally begets blood:

> Martín was in the garden
> digging . . . .
>
> . . . . . .
>
> . . . . when frozen
> in horror was his blood.
> The spade that in the earth he drove
> blood stained appeared when he drew it forth.

In contrast the youngest brother, Miguel, enriched and strengthened in a foreign land, labors with a good will and receives an abundant reward:

> The colonist with faith and will
> to till the soil bent his strength
>
> . . . . .
>
> Now with golden kernels ripe
> wheat crowns the field,
> in the land which Miguel sowed
> and fertile summer chose to bless.

In "La tierra de Alvargonzález" the other miracle of spring sought in the poet's reflections on his dying wife becomes a fact and nature rewards Miguel, while Martin and Juan commit suicide in the dark lake—the unknown and remote sea transformed into a familiar but feared lagoon.

In the poem Miguel is not slain, partly because, as Allen Phillips points out, this second crime contributes neither to the tale's unity nor to the retribution required of the murderers and exacted in their suicide.[28] More important, the contrast between Miguel and his brother is heightened: not only do his fields bear fruit while theirs remain barren, but he lives to enjoy his father's land. Machado envisions the death of the brothers as directly redeeming the land, and as Miguel's efforts meet a response in the land, so the land also reflects the retribution exacted for crime.

The ballad is a hopeful poem, concluded in imagery of abundant summer and in symbols suggestive of reward and hopes fulfilled. But the hopes voiced in "Campos de Castilla" proved vain for Spain and the shadow of Cain was a more accurate symbol. By 1936 civil war had launched national fratricide throughout the country. Writing from Valencia in 1938, Machado turns in memory toward Soria and asks:

Tell me, martial plane, if the Duero high
where journey you, its poet can recall
or does, once more, over the planet fall
Cain's shadow, pest of war, in shadow where you fly?[29]

Even before he speaks he knows the answer to his question. The years of war constitute the fruits of evil, prefigured in the sterile fields of Alvargonzález. The images of spring, once clear symbols of hope, are reversed in order to portray destruction:

Spirits of cowardice and hate run loose,
fell trees which crowned your groves and chop
their wood, trample your golden wine press crop
and crush the grain your fields produce.[30]

Although not a prophecy of civil war, "La tierra de Alvargonzález" exemplifies the evils engendered by base passions as well as the national apathy which reproduces itself in a continuing spiritual void. But despair is not Machado's response. Images of dawn, of day reborn to a new challenge, express his awareness of those who share his dream of a vital, dynamic Spain:

And yet another Spain is being born
the Spain of chisel and of mace,
with that eternal youth which labors sworn
to build from ageless heritage of race.[31]

But this future, rising like a phoenix from the past, is only a portion of the poet's total vision. Because his personal hopes and his temporal preoccupations are equally encircled by hope and despair, he recognizes, as he regards his nation, that the future is also menaced by a moribund past and the lethargy it begets:

There is a Spaniard who would choose
to live and who to live begins
between that Spain which, dead, must lose
and that which, yawning, never wins.

Young Spaniard who now strains
to be, in this world may God defend.
One of those long damned Spain
will freeze your heart and be your end.[32]

This implicit peril is all the more real for Machado because of the unfulfilled ideals of his own generation:

In depth of all our dreams—with this
inheritance of dying century which never glory had displayed—
to welcome dawn we then did strive and with
our discontent the light of great ideas battle made.

But each his road of madness personal pursued,
limbered his arm as for the fight, his valour fine
did show; polished his armour to be viewed
and said: Today is evil but tomorrow will be mine.

And that tomorrow now has come. . . . All Spain
in dirty trappings of the Carnival arrayed
remains, poor, squalid, drunken, vain;
her wound's own blood her wine has made.

Yet later generation of our youth,
if the higher pinnacle to you is lure,
go to your venture, transparent to the truth,
clear as diamond is and as the diamond pure.[33]

In this poem of national concern and challenge to his countrymen, as in "El pasado efímero" and "El mañana efímero,"[34] Machado seeks to communicate his ideas directly rather than to evoke them through images of the Castilian landscape as, for example, in "A orillas del Duero" or, less completely, in "La tierra de Alvargonzález."

The dawn of a new Spain is a more conventional metaphor than the dawns of Machado's dream-oriented poems. Still he employs the image of dreams to convey an as yet unrealized future, similar to the unfulfillment and hope which coexist in his autobiographical poems. Reality reveals only the ill effects of the past upon the present; the dream makes possible, irrationally, a generation which may overcome its negative inheritance.

The Generation, however, is an intellectually realistic group. And the idealist—be he Unamuno, Ganivet, Azorín, Machado—is trapped by his dreams, since they presuppose no practical goal, plan or definite system. For the men of this generation to agree upon an end would be to invalidate individual thought; to conform to a practical means would be to betray their own vision of absolute personal liberty. Only in dreams and in poetic symbols are their goals adequately expressed.

The poem, "In the depth of all our dreams," resumes the paradoxes of the Generation's visions. Exaltation of the individual and distrust of political and social creeds produce a tension between action and idealism. Unamuno issues a call for dedication to a goal shrouded in doubt and irrationality; Baroja attacks philosophic and political systems without offering an alternative theory; Azorín observes that action destroys meditation but that ideas are not fruitful without action. It is above all this concept of human will dissipated in a struggle between the theoretical and practical which Machado describes. Machado recognizes that, in spite of nobility, fervor, and an apparent capacity to accomplish great things, he and his contemporaries have yet to join battle in behalf of effective, tangible change. "All Spain / in dirty trappings of the Carnival arrayed / remains."

The dawn to which the dreams aspire remains speculative, still on the threshold of reality. Therefore, when Machado addresses a new generation, it is with a challenge to real creative effort directed toward a clear and certain goal ("transparent to the truth"), a goal they themselves must shape. But the poet does single out the condition upon which all effort and all success depends: the human will ("if the higher pinnacle to you is lure / go to your venture . . .").

Machado is not, of course, accusing his contemporaries of accomplishing nothing. The less imagistic the poem, the more Machado tends to deal, as here, in theories of national failure. His hope is tied to symbols drawn from the landscape, not to theory. Speculative interpretations, in contrast to nature, offer no solace.

When he discusses each of his contemporaries he does so in a more positive spirit and, significantly, in images of the countryside which recall his memories of Soria and his hopes for both a human and a natural spring. Thus his response to Azorín's book *Castilla* is first a vision of the landscape as both a physical and a spiritual entity and then an expression of his hopes for the revitalization of Spain:

> With the melancholy of your word
> all Castile to my room has come,
> Castile gentle or bold is heard,
> arid Castile under la Mancha's sun,
> where down to sea the rivers long of Spain
> still run, that never yet have seen the sea,
> Castile of the high and noble barren plain,
> Castile of the ageless black oak tree.
>
> . . . . .
>
> . . . . Azorín, I do believe
> in the subtle soul of your Castile.
> And from a land that fasting makes and fun
>
> . . . . .
>
> I with you in liberty believe and hope
> and in the faith that's born
> when man for God will seek but not achieve
> and in the God that you create and form.
>
> . . . . .
>
> Oh listen, Azorín and hear. Spain's will
> would be to rise, to soar; a new Spain to create.

And shall she perish in the old Spain's chill?
Shall she be strangled in the old Spain's fate?
To save the new Epiphany must we
respond, the hour is born,
with ax and fire to the new day loyal be.
Hear the cocks salute the coming of the morn.[35]

Similar in some respects to the direct challenge of more outspoken national poems and in others to the evocation of Castile through familiar details and symbols of Castilian character, the poem for Azorín unites image and ideology. In the stern countenance of the landscape, in austere images typical of Castile, both the strength and the poverty of the nation are reflected. But vision and interpretation are not enough, the poet concludes, calling directly for intervention in Spain's future. And this summons is identical with the image of dawn, for the cocks' call inevitably announces a new day. The promise is in nature, the potential in man. The two visions compliment one another, each making the other possible.

Only one of these visions is the familiar evocation of hope and memory through nature; transformed, that concept of the world is present even in Machado's most political or outspoken poems. In addition to the groups of images described earlier, in discussing Spain Machado makes particular use of other images: rocks, crags and mountains; cities, herbs and other plants. The names are new but the functions familiar.

The mountains, already present in the frequent references to Moncayo and Espino in the poems referring to Leonor, suggest relative permanence. They are the *tempo lento* against which temporal change in the nation is noted. They function as do the fountains in Sevillan patios, as forms of temporal continuity. But they also change. If the water that gives life is also the river rushing to the sea, the mountains for all their endurance are also worn by time. One of the poet's starkest acknowledgments of time is the reference in "A orillas del Duero" to the changing mountains: "All things must change, flow on, journey, flee or cycle make; / the sea and hill are changed. . . ."

Cities too are links with the national past. They display, especially in the poems describing Soria, past grandeur reduced to decay and misery. They suggest the pride which memory engenders in a nation with no present right to pride. They are the physical counterparts of the symbolic rags in which Machado portrays his country.

And while cities fall into ruin and even mountains erode, the sturdy Castilian herbs flower each spring, a few daisies spring up. The plants and herbs of the landscape are, above all, emblematic of the tenacious character of the people, bearing witness both to the best in the Castilian farmer—elsewhere portrayed more bleakly—and to the cyclical renaissance in nature.

These images are part, then, of the ambivalent world of loss and anticipation, here as elsewhere embodied in images of water, roads and cycles of changing day and changing season. The Duero is both a highway to the sea and the source of life in the Castilian valley. It occupies the most significant line of the poem "A orillas del Duero," uniting physical and symbolic visions as it crosses the heart, both literal and imagistic, of Iberia.

The poplar-lined roads, which serve as symbols for the poet's vision of life, are evoked as facets of the harsh countryside. His use of the day-night contrast is, as we have noted, usually a traditional vision of dawn as hopeful future. In "A orillas del Duero" however, the passage from afternoon to evening parallels a movement from present to past and back to the present. Here the night is not a negative image standing in contrast to dawn. But roads and dawn can also form part of a dream. And if the dream dialogue for Spain is less specifically articulated than the personal vision of "Los sueños dialogados," it is no less present in repeated references to his dream and to those of his contemporaries.

The dream fulfilled is most often evoked through images of spring. Life returning to the countryside about Soria, intimately related to images of spring rain, tangibly implies the future still latent in a hollow present. When these images figure in the Civil War poems as touchstones of destruction the horror is intensified because it is nature which reflects life and which is, in war, reduced to death.

But one vain spring and one slaughtered harvest do not suggest despair, for the life of nature is a life in cycle, a good world, as the poet writes, to be born again.[36] Machado's most specific application of the dream vision and of spring to the national theme is found in a eulogy for his teacher, Francisco Giner de los Ríos, founder of the Instituto Libre de Enseñanza. Because of the Instituto's importance to the entire Generation of '98, the elegy for don Francisco is properly more than a personal tribute. It is also the acceptance of his challenge and a participation in his vision of renaissance through the tangible reality of Castile:

> Since the master now is gone,
> the morning light spoke
> and said: Three days past
> my brother Francis ceased his work.
> Then is he dead?—We know only
> that by a clear road he took his leave
> bidding us what we should do: Make
> for my requiem a grief of labor and of hope.
> Be good, no more; be as I among you
> have sought to be: your soul.
> Live then, for life goes on.
> The dead are dead; the shadows pass.
> He who remains, keep faith with he who lived before.
> Let anvil sound and mourning bell be still.

And toward another purer light
departed he who brother was to dawn,
as sun within the craftsman's shop
the old man with the joy of life complete.
—Yes, bear his body, oh my friends,
to the blue mountains bear him then,
to the blue-tipped peaks
of lofty Guadarrama range.
There the deep crevices are found,
where amid green pine the wind entones.
May his heart rest
beneath an ancient oak,
in land where grows the thyme, where sport
the golden butterflies.
There one day past the master did
dream yet another flowering of Spain.[37]

Giner's ideals and the example of his work issue a challenge to Machado and his countrymen, and the poet responds to and echoes this challenge. All that will be—and can be—accomplished depends ultimately, he believes, upon this man's vision. His has been both an immediate influence and a permanent inspiration: the poet addresses him as master for he was both literally a teacher and the author of a philosophy of life, as brother of the light of dawn, since to illumine knowledge and understanding was his goal as an educator and the dawn of a changed, awakened and vital nation, his goal as a lover of his country. Machado refers to his death without a sense of finality since his achievement and his example survive.

No less than his teacher the poet knows that everything passes: life, joy and sorrow, and lament. Only one's toil and one's hope endure, for they are constantly recreated. Thus to mourn is not enough; sorrow must beget the will to act ("Let anvil sound and mourning bell be still"). In the act of homage and respectful burial, Giner's followers must also take up his vision. The poet can wish rest for his dead teacher in the midst of the pure, austere beauty of Castile, with its tenacious herbs and innocent beauty, because he and others continue to work on behalf of that land. Thus he turns to Giner's dreams, concluding his elegy with a hope still to be fulfilled.

Machado's vision of Castile—her wretched present, the glories of her past, her pride, her stark, austere beauty, her potential for rebirth—reflects the same awareness of time and sense of rapport between the physical and spiritual worlds as appears in his most personal poems. The elements stressed may be different but many of the same images recur with similar or identical functions. As particulars of the landscape embody memories and hopes, they also suggest national accomplishments and national decadence, as well as Spain's most notable virtues and vices. Dignity, seriousness and severity are mirrored in the rocky hills and the unchanging Guadarrama; perseverance in the multiple herbs of fields and hillsides; humility and firmness in the Castilian oak.

But the dry plains also echo human hatred, pettiness and apathy. In images of this countryside the poet expresses both the Generation of '98's ideas and the results of his own experience. Conscious of temporality, with the constant change it imposes upon man and nature, Machado sees the present as part of a total vision encompassing both the past and future.

Machado does not seek to give Spain a new soul, to change her intrinsically, even if this were possible. He portrays, rather, his ideal as a reawakening of the spirit of don Quijote, as a new flowering in images of spring come to the familiar Castilian landscape.

Conclusion

THE EXPRESSION of human temporal conditions, individual and national, through images of nature reflects an effort subjectively to project life, imperfectly conceived into the world perceived and known. Nature itself witnesses the passage of time, not only in the life of man—birth, change and death—but also in its own varying tempos: the almost imperceptible alteration of the landscape, the rapid succession of days and seasons, and in its cycles, which constantly afford new beginnings. In this interplay of swift and gradual change, Machado grasps the multiple and often paradoxical relationships which link the past, the present and the future.

Nature both imposes the limits of temporal experience, defining that which we call present, and goes beyond these boundaries. Because some things are relatively enduring—trees, rocks, mountain peaks, fountains, old cities—it is possible, from the vantage point of a particular moment, to evoke experiences formerly associated with them. At time's other margin, rebirth in nature communicates a substantial form to the poet's desires for the restoration of things lost but still remembered, transcendence over death and finite understanding, and the spiritual renaissance of Spain.

Within the images suggested by water, roads and the cycles of day and year, Machado observes both existence and transition, the visible counterparts of his simultaneous awareness of being and temporality. Thus is he able to articulate a vision of personal memories and hopes, describing a spiritual landscape by means of the particulars of the physical. On the other hand, speaking of his country, he is primarily concerned with a direct statement of his ideas, clarified and illustrated through metaphors drawn from nature and through an evocation of the Spanish countryside.

Conscious that water, in various forms, is indicative both of genesis and movement, Machado envisions rain, rivers and similar images as expressive of life's creative, transitional and destructive aspects. Grief, descending like rain upon the events of life, fathers human sensitivity and intensifies experience, while love is its fulfillment. Yet neither grief nor love is eternal. Moments of youthful joy, of pleasure, even of melancholy pass, their transiency sensed and their memory evoked against a background of impassive monotony, the ever-gushing stone fountains. Life itself is constantly in flight, like a river rushing to the sea, destined for an end it does not and cannot know. But the poet is not resigned to extinction or to ignorance. His memories and his hopes are a protest against time and a desire to transcend this unknown sea, confronting the inability to believe and the acknowledged limitations of finite intelligence. His is not a conviction about life, but a struggle, a question and a doubt.

To doubt is not to despair, but to continue, always rejecting simple and superficial interpretations of life while continually searching for truth. Primarily, Machado rejects man's journey through life as a real and definite road. On the contrary, as he travels each man is obliged to create his own path; the future does not exist and only the past is known, imperfectly. So too the poet, as he searches, possesses only recollections, images from which to create a visible, although subjective, future. Ultimately, his search confronts the same enigma implicit in the image of the river fleeing to the sea, where he snatches from the mystery itself the same vague hope. Confessing that memories, doubt and sorrow haunt his path, the poet nevertheless affirms his dedication to seek truth, as long as there is an uncertainty in which to seek.

But since the future is an object of speculation and only the past is known, the poet finds himself always at a moment of finality: his is a vision of afternoons, of life approaching its limit. The dawn is a dream which, for man as for nature, may perhaps lie beyond the barrier of night.

Dreaming affords an illusion of possession, but the necessity of waking terminates all dreams. From life's finite illusion of reality man must wake one day, and the poet, who has described himself as surrounded by uncertainty, confesses that he has no solution to the riddle of existence. For all that man perceives with spiritual vision is shadowed by a temporal perspective—by memories as well as by hopes. The vision which Machado constantly pursues—an understanding of life in its totality, entirely apart from time—is wrapt in shadow. Thus, says the poem on the death of Abel Martín, to die is to encounter the unknown, to penetrate pure shadow.

Human existence is a unique journey, neither revealing nor promising rebirth. In contrast, nature reveals myriad rebirths toward which the poet's longing turns. Throughout the landscape, the first white flowers of spring evoke innocence, youth, joy and love restored; the trees' new foliage witnesses a return of vitality and beauty and harbors the same birds' song heard in years past; and bees go about their creative, transforming labor. Faced with this renaissance, Machado dreams that for himself, as for the physical world, youthful innocence and joy may be restored, and the past, with its sorrows and regret, transformed into a beneficent future. Yet these are, he knows, attainments of a dream reality. Just as he acknowledges that his desire to understand life, to possess truth and to attain the certainty of transcending death, is frustrated by his own finite being, he recognizes that his vision of a human renaissance is a purely subjective one, an image projected beyond the limitations of existence. But even as an image it is the only vision he knows in which the fear of death can be overcome, the presence of Leonor felt, and an enduring life—an eternal spring—prophesied.

Thus memories, hopes and images of the physical world are facets of the poet's dialogue with time. The obscurity in which he finds himself, however, and the impermanence of all things lead him to doubt the reality of the dialogue. For conversation requires a something or a someone entirely independent of the speaker. And if only appearances and interpretations exist, then there is no objective reality: no one to whom the poet can address himself: nothing which is not bound to his finitude and, therefore, doomed to expire with it. The dialogue itself becomes a doubt, in which Machado turns first to the object of his memory, Leonor; then to the landscape, visible and present; to his hope and fear; and, finally, in the last sonnet of "Los sueños dialogados," to the enigma of reality: that alone which he perceives as existing independent of himself. Because he continues to question, his words do not suggest despair, but desire.

Similarly, aware of Spain's vanquished glories, of her physical and spiritual decay, of her apathy, base passions and empty pride, he does not resign himself to the defects of contemporary society but rather desires that his nation be transformed and challenges his countrymen to join in the task of accomplishing that transformation. Just as his life and personal hopes are influenced by memories, his concept of Spain is shaped by a historical dimension. Contrasting and comparing the past and the present he is able to epitomize the spirit of Spain: "Miserable Castile who yesterday did reign / wrapt now in rags what you know not you disdain."

A participant in, rather than a disinterested observor of this spirit, Machado feels that sincere love for his country which both admits and deplores her weaknesses and vices. His disgust is a prophecy that a hollow society will engender only more hollowness, and that hatred, greed and jealousy—the shadow of Cain—will reap a harvest of blood. But he also finds among his contemporaries a few men who share his dreams and his desire for a better Spain and through whose efforts and example this desire can be fulfilled.

On behalf of his country and on his own behalf, the poet confronts time, desiring to understand perfectly, desiring to transcend finite existence. Although recognizing that he is always frustrated by the passage of time, which makes all knowledge relative and confirms finitude in death, he continues to search: remembering, hoping and dreaming and, ultimately, acknowledging that the search can have no end save an encounter with the enigma of death itself, when, for him, time will cease to be.

Implicit in the theme of temporality and in its representation through images of nature are the poet's approach—speculative and personal—to experience, his conception of change in man and nature, his poetic world wherein this conception is expressed, his view of the relationship between periods of time and his concern for the certainty or uncertainty of all human knowledge.

Since into a poet's vision enter, directly or indirectly, all aspects of his personality, Machado frequently expresses himself as philosopher in poems. Before the inevitable passage of time, he believes, the roles of poet and philosopher fuse. "Some day," says Mairena to his students, "the role of philosopher and poet will be interchanged. The poets will sing of their surprise before metaphysical truth and the philosophers will little by little mute their violas to relate . . . the *fugit irreparabile tempus.* . . . And thus will the poet and philosopher be face to face, never hostile."[1] In anticipation of that day Machado's poems penetrate the realm of universal concepts; they question the nature of man, his struggle with time and with truth; and investigate the character of emotion, reason and memory.

Yet his poetry remains autobiographical, the song of places known well, of experiences remembered, and of personal responses to life. But Machado is not the poet of two distinct phases: the one personal, the other speculative. Embodying Unamuno's belief that a philosophic system is indivisible from the person of the philosopher, Machado fuses individual experience and universal theme in a single vision. Thus when he asks "What is it to die?" he is concerned with his own fate and with the concept of death as applied to all men. And when he strives to reconcile that which is mutable and that which is enduring in life, he speaks both of his own memories, regrets, wishes and dreams and of the essence of being.

In the daily process of living, as in metaphysics, change itself evidences a dual character: destructive and repetitive. Both nature and man proclaim this duality: destruction evidenced physically in ruins and spiritually in human awareness of time's passing; recurrence, visibly manifested in dawn and spring and subjectively in memory and hope. For Machado memories, even as they confirm his sense of loss and of solitude, imply a more enduring existence than that of the momentary present. By recreating a tangible object, they repeat, however imperfectly, the past.

Thus memory provides a physical bond between one period of time and another. Only because he is able to reenter the past in recollections is man conscious of continuity, deprivation and fulfillment in the present. From his own past the poet learns grief and disappointment, but also the persistence of love and life's creative spirit. In Spain's history, resplendent with conquests and accomplishments, he reads an indictment of contemporary social and spiritual stagnation as well as recognizes his country's capacity for new achievements and recaptured greatness.

It is this sense of continuity which begets hope and the sense of loss which engulfs all hopes in fear and doubt. To the formless future the poet communicates the form of things enduring and things remembered. In the light of sunset he sees the light of dawn; in recollections of Sorian spring, the figure of his dead wife; in the rewakened Guardarrama, a new flowering of Spain. So too his dreams borrow the appearance of reality from his memories, creating an illusion of possession and of permanence.

The illusion is at once a romantic trait, a mythic pattern and, as such, a bond with poetic schools and movements far removed from the Generation of '98 or Hispanic literature. Machado is in certain ways a neoromantic, closer to English than to Spanish romanticism; a formal rather than an extemporizing poet, one whose romanticism makes no pretense to new visions; and an archetypal poet whose myth is nature, viewed not as a sympathetic force but as the reality which yields symbols.

In theme and style his voice resembles many poets of the nineteenth and twentieth centuries. A poet-philosopher, his closest spiritual affinity is with Hölderlin who recognizes with Machado that the two functions are complimentary but opposite voices of the same vision and that, as the German poet phrases it, "the poet and the philosopher dwell close together on mountains far apart."

That Machado the philosopher is a romantic offers no contradiction, for his romanticism supposes a world-view, personal at the outset, formal in mid-career, and apocalyptic in the late poems. As a cosmic poet he is both less ambitious than Espronceda or Coleridge and more absolute. His myths are few and primordial and his cosmos is totally contained in the cycle of death and resurrection.

Toward the end of his career the world-view becomes prophetic and the images less predictable. However, because his sources are almost entirely Spanish or, in a few instances, Hellenic, his prophetic poems only vaguely suggest Blake with whom, in technique and his interpretation of man, he seems to have much in common. Closer to the *Songs of Innocence and Experience* than to the *Prophetic Books*, particularly in *Campos de Castilla* and *Nuevas Canciones*, Machado is also a poet less certain than Blake of his cosmos.

Yet he is in the English sense a romantic, a poet of the dichotomy of order and chaos (the prevalent mood of "Otro clima"), of the desert and the sea, and of search and uncertainty. Nature is Machado's order as is time: the former is a positive structure because cyclical and the latter, negative because irreversible. Machado's desert is Castile, la Mancha, the parched Spain which is both the romantic world and a historic and contemporary reality. His sea is the universal unknown and also the most Spanish of references: the sea whence lead our lives in the life's long dying. In the romantic tradition there are no rules for his search. Nor are there answers for his questions.

In this fulfillment of the romantic commitment he is close to only one Spanish romantic, Espronceda, who himself recalls English romanticism rather than his own contemporaries. In spite of his familiarity with French poetry and his visits to Paris, Machado has almost nothing in common with formal French romanticism. Machado's nature is ritual and the god whom ritual acknowledges, a law unto itself. Nature reassures man that perhaps his hopes are not altogether in vain. This is no pathetic fallacy in the usual sense, not a simple reflection of human feelings in the natural world. Neither is Machado's nature a philosophic verification, as for Wordsworth. For Machado nature is prior to philosophy and so can, perhaps, save man from his own reason.

It is best to call Machado a romantic corrupted by reason. In many, although certainly not in all respects, his romanticism parallels Auden's discussion of the romantic spirit in *The Enchafèd Flood* in that he views the sea as the relevant expression of life and the voyage as man's proper state; in judging the present as a polemical situation in which Spain's apathy and former pride stand in radical juxtaposition; in his god, who is precisely the immanent god of self-awareness—as Auden phrases it, "the ego's consciousness of itself as self-contained, as embracing all of which it is aware in a unity of experience"; in his vision of nature as life, in his quixotic quest, and in his self-consciousness, which is both a movement from self and a quest for what and who one is.[2]

In almost all of these romantic realities Machado collides with his own training as a philosopher. If he discovered Heidegger late in life, he had been trained by Bergson as early as 1911 and used Kant as part of "Poema de un día" in the second edition of *Campos de Castilla.* The ticking clock of "Poema de un día" and of briefer poems, the verbal games Juan de Mairena plays with Leibniz' monad, and the jesting references to Bergson and Kant are tragicomic ways of coping with the dichotomy.

Ultimately the poet finds that he cannot cope. *Nuevas canciones* and the *Cancionero apócrifo* increasingly become collections of contradictions: the romantic's faith in the individual and the rational need for a viable conclusion; a desire to know himself (the "to be what I have never been / one") and his inquiry into the nature of death, confronting questions about the reality outside of self. "Los sueños dialogados" concludes "be I whoever I may be," for the more vital issue is to know with whom the dialogue is made.

This emphasis by Machado, almost in spite of himself, on his role as trained academician distinguishes him from the French symbolists and from Baudelaire with whom he has, nonetheless, much in common. Unlike the formal romantics of early nineteenth-century France but like Baudelaire, Machado inhabits a human world without order, whose muse is personal, evocative, antirational and prophetic, a world in which illogic is as valid as logic.

The dream-dialogue invocation to loneliness—"Tell me with whom my dialogue is made"—recalls Baudelaire's confrontation with sorrow, "Ma doleur, donne-moi la main." Both feel and objectify in art the mystery and the anguish of being human. And both live in a world whose standards they cannot accept.

But the Generation's argument with Spain is more quixotic than fin-de-siècle. Berating apathy and false pride, Machado, recognizing the shortcomings of his own era, forever articulates a hope for tomorrow. For Machado nothing is ever at an end; everything is in process.

Poetry too is process, an evolving reality. Like Baudelaire, Machado is conceptually and verbally, rather than metrically, experimental. His major poems include octosyllables, handecasyllables, one long alexandrine and a sonnet sequence. His free verse and metric experiments are infrequent and not always successful. Borrowing perhaps directly from Baudelaire or more probably from the modernists—whose artistic ancestors were at least fifty per cent French—Machado employs a mingling of sensory imagery. Dawn *sounds* in the East; the crash of waves on the surrealistic shore of "Otro clima" is *green*; the uncertain *white word* ascends from an April fife. The perceived world is altered by our impressions of it and communicated simultaneously as world and as human impression.

The validity of the reaction is that which remains absolute for the romantic and always in question for Machado. He may write to Unamuno that for him Leonor lives and he feels certain of finding her again. But the subjective *again* is as much desperate hope as personal certitude. In this respect Machado is more properly a mythic than a romantic poet. His myths are the cycle and the quest. If the quest is fulfilled, then all truth is cyclic. But Machado never affirms that much. "Y no es verdad, dolor" ends with the affirmation of search: "thus do I . . . ever seek for God amid the mist," and the *Cancionero apócrifo* concludes with an image of shadow and the vague distant ribbon of a road.

As a quest poet, Machado is oriented toward past and future. His concern with both his own past and with Spanish history corresponds to the epic nostalgia for a lost golden age and don Quijote's mock-epic nostalgia for a golden age which never was. His vision of dawn, spring and a renascent Spain are his Grail, vaguer than the immortality which Unamuno spells out as the end of his quest. First he seeks to find himself and, therefore, makes a romantic quest; then he seeks his partner in dialogue, thus pursuing a philosophic truth, an assurance of reality independent of himself.

As a human pursuit the quest is unfulfilled. For Machado neither the return to Eden nor the renunciation of the dream is possible. In consequence he is an intentionally inconclusive poet. Despairing romantics know that they despair and visionary romantics affirm at least their vision. For Machado everything is problematical.

The only way out of the maze is, of course, that which nature offers. The poem as archetype is reality: specifically, as Northrop Frye distinguishes between the poem seen as permanent because structural and the poem which "in its archetypal phase . . . imitates nature not (as in the formal phase) nature as a structure or system but nature as a cyclical process."[3]

This juxtaposition of human inconclusiveness and the absolute cycles of nature remotely recalls Wordsworth and, indeed, Hopkins. Finally, however, Machado is concerned with the archetypes as such, just as he is—logically—interested in the monad of Leibniz: both give him a structural unity and, simultaneously, an absolute.

With his considerable debt to the modernists and through them to the French symbolists, and his rapport with romanticism, Machado's poetic world is oriented more toward the nineteenth than the twentieth century. Nevertheless he has recently been an inspiration and model for the contemporary generation, not the protest poetry of one contemporary school but the nostalgic, evocative poems which reflect the other face of contemporary Spain.

When *Cuadernos Hispanoamericanos* dedicated an issue to Machado, it was to the young poets that they turned: Bo, Cano, Luis Rosales, Valverde. Cano and the poet-critic Bousoño have been two of his most astute interpreters and those who have concerned themselves with the writings and ideology of youth—Dámaso Alonso, José Luis Aranguren, Julián Marías—have written impressive studies.

However, little immediate rapport with or influence upon the poets succeeding the Generation of '98 is to be found. Guillén's quest for pure poetry, the abstraction and expressionist symbolism of Aleixandre, the sophisticated primitivism of Lorca, and the metric experiment by almost everyone are dictated by different aesthetic principles.

For similar reasons it is difficult to relate Machado meaningfully to the major English and American poets of the twentieth century. Yet Machado resembles Wallace Stevens in the intellectual tenor of his work, the degree to which speculative considerations and philosophic problems inform the publications of both. Occasionally, in *Nuevas Canciones* and frequently in the *Cancionero apócrifo*, Machado's imagery becomes difficult and esoteric. The deceptive simplicity of Stevens' work parallels Machado's own use, in other poems, of apparently simple images such as clocks or a child's rocking horse, and distillation of thought characterizes the work of both poets.

But essentially Machado is more time-haunted than any writer of recent decades. His temporal consciousness dates from the same age which produced—not by accident—*A la recherche du temps perdu.* Machado too has gone in search of time lost and, except for his own definition (the dialogue with time), no phrase is more descriptive of his work than Proust's title. For Machado, as for Proust, reality is a delicately sustained web of time, interwoven and self-sustaining.

The future is erected upon the structure of the past; the past interpreted in the light of the present; the present suspended between memory and loss, hope and fear. Experiences overlap and blend into one another, each retaining its independent identity; time is never whole for Machado, yet all its individual moments influence one another, shadowing, constantly altering, falsifying, and illuminating, like the broken, changing colors in a prism. From the poet's intense awareness of these temporal relationships are born his other voices, Abel Martín and Juan de Mairena.

Each of these alter egos possesses a distinct existence with its definite limits, yet each reaches beyond these limits in his influence: Martín upon Mairena; Mairena upon Machado. They belong to a larger vision of time than that which any man's life comprehends. Thus the poet affirms, tentatively and personally, his freedom from the present, for together with his alter egos, he is able to live simultaneously in three temporal conditions. Fully conscious that they are nothing but specters of his own thought, Machado nevertheless creates in them two beings whose reality is his own but whose existence he defends as independent.

But they cannot speak to one another. Potential dramatis personae in the poet's dialogue, neither Martín nor Mairena can converse with the other nor with his author. Each speaks singly, bound by his temporal circumstances, while in the total context which spans their three lives, no voice is heard.

All things which lie outside the poet's subjectivity, individual or historical, are silent except as created by the collective effort of particular consciences: "All forms of objectivity or appearances of what is objective are . . . products of de-subjectivizing . . . an illusion of objectivity, of being which is not being . . . the shadow of being."[4] If this is true, then nothing is real, neither man's ideas nor his concepts, hopes, or memories, not even the physical world. All experience is haunted by uncertainty: love is creative, but its world exists only for the lovers. Dreams, also creative, are no more than illusions. Even the mind encounters barriers, frustrating its efforts to penetrate the domain of wisdom. And since the mind intervenes in man's understanding of the sensory world, nature itself ultimately becomes a subjective vision. Thus, Machado concludes: "insecurity, uncertainty, doubt are, perhaps, our only truths."[5] But, even in this, faithful to his doubt, he is not sure.

Temporality is responsible for this inconclusiveness since it permits only a fragmentary understanding, snatching away one moment's perception with the onset of the next, but leaving the shadows of memory and expectation to obscure the present. Hence the poet feels himself able to affirm only uncertainty and illusion: there is no road for life's journey; no solution for the enigma encountered in death; no peace in finite existence; and neither clarity nor guidance for one seeking truth.

As a philosopher Machado is drawn toward the conclusion that no reality exists apart from his own existence and that all things are finite, their doom identical with his own. As a poet, he embraces emotions and irrational hopes in conflict with doubt, as well as the visible world, which does not speak to the mind alone. Being both poet and philosopher, he doubts and denies without despair. Confessing his finite limitations, the obscurity of human understanding, and the uncertainty of absolute truth, he continues to desire, intensely but irrationally, transcendence over time—and hence over death—and a vision of reality, independent and integral. This desire is implicit in his continuing search, in the portrayal of death not as destruction but as mystery, in images of continuity beyond annihilation and, above all, in the act of demanding from uncertainty itself the meaning of the dialogue with time.

For one who knows, intuitively, as well as intellectually, that his dialogue is carried on in a dream, the act of waking represents the critical moment toward which all his doubts and hopes tend. Culminating in uncertainty, in the mystery which he cannot solve, Machado's question continually repeats itself in the world of its birth, in a vision of the poet's life and of familiar landscapes. Through this vision the question is also answered—neither absolutely nor philosophically—in the reality created by each poem.

Appendix: Spanish Text of Poems

Nature as an Expression of Temporality

1. "And it is not true, sorrow, I know / you well"

Y no es verdad, dolor, yo to conozco,
tú eres nostalgia de la vida buena,
y soledad del corazón sombrío,
de barco sin naufragio y sin estrella.

Como perro olvidado que no tiene
huella ni olfato y yerra
por los caminos, sin camino, como
el niño que en la noche de una fiesta

se pierde entre el gentío
y el aire polvoriento y las candelas
chispeantes, atónito, y asombra
su corazón de música y de pena,

así voy yo, borracho, melancólico,
guitarrista lunático, poeta
y pobre hombre en sueños,
siempre buscando a Dios entre la niebla.

Images and Cycles

2. "April contains a thousand rains"

Son de abril las aguas mil.
Sopla el viento achubascado,
y entre nublado y nublado
hay trozos de cielo añil.

Agua y sol. El iris brilla.
En una nube lejana,
zigzaguea
una centella amarilla.

La lluvia da en la ventana
y el cristal repiquetea.

A través de la neblina
que forma la lluvia fina,
se divisa un prado verde,
y en encinar se esfumina,
y una sierra gris se pierde.

Los hilos del aguacero
sesgan las nacientes frondas,
y agitan las turbias ondas
en el remanso del Duero.

Lloviendo está en los haberes
y en las pardas sementeras;
hay sol en los encinares,
charcos por las carreteras.

Lluvia y sol. Ya se obscurece
el campo, ya se ilumina;
allí un cerro desparece,
allá surge una colina.

Ya son claros, ya sombríos
los dispersos caseríos,
los lejanos torreones.

Hacia la sierra plomiza
van rodando en pelotones
nubes de guata y ceniza.

3. "Good tears once spilled"

¡Buenas lágrimas vertidas
por un amor juvenil,
cual frescas lluvias caídas
sobre los campos de abril!

. . . . .

lágrimas que alegremente
brotabais como en la fuente
las limpias aguas sonoras.

4. "Yesterday poet, today poor and sad"

Poeta ayer, hoy triste y pobre
filósofo trasnochado,
tengo en monedas de cobre
el oro de ayer cambiado.

5. "The valley roads to river go"

Los caminos del valle van al río
y allí, junto del agua, amor espera.
¿Por ti se ha puesto el campo ese atavío
de joven, oh invisible compañera?

. . . . .

eres tú quien florece y resucita.

6. "You, lovers, woven are of spring"

Tejidos sois de primavera, amantes,
de tierra y agua y viento y sol tejidos.
La sierra en vuestro pechos jadeantes,
en los ojos los campos florecidos.

7. "In a garden I have dreamed of you"

En un jardín te he soñado,
alto, Guiomar, sobre el río,
jardín de un tiempo cerrado
con verjas de hierro frío.

Un ave insólito canta
en el almez, dulcemente,
junto al agua viva y santa,
toda sed y toda fuente.

En ese jardín, Guiomar,
el mutuo jardín que inventan
dos corazones al par,
se funden y complementan
nuestras horas. . . .

8. "The fountain water's flight"

. . . . . La fuente vertía
sobre el blanco mármol su monotonía.

La fuente cantaba: ¿Te recuerda, hermano,
un sueño lejano mi canto presente?
Fue una tarde lenta del lento verano.

. . . . . .

—Fue esta misma tarde: mi cristal vertía
como hoy sobre el mármol su montonía.

. . . . . .

[poeta] Cuéntame mi alegre leyenda olvidada.

—Yo no sé leyendas de antigua alegría,
sino historias viejas de melancolía.

. . . . . .

Dijeron tu pena tus labios que ardían:
la sed que ahora tienen, entonces tenían.

9. "I listen to the song"

Yo escucho los cantos
de viejas cadencias,
que los niños cantan

. . . . . .

Las canciones llevan
confusa la historia
y clara la pena;
como clara el agua
lleva su conseja
de viejos amores,
que nunca se cuentan.

. . . . . .

La fuente de piedra
vertía su eterno
cristal de leyenda.

. . . . . .

Seguía su cuento
la fuente serena,
borrada la historia
contaba la pena.

10. "It was a night in May"

Era una noche del mes
de mayo, azul y serena.
Sobre el agudo ciprés
brillaba la luna llena,

iluminando la fuente
en donde el agua surtía
sollozando intermitente.
Sólo la fuente se oía.

. . . . . .

Y una dulce melodía
vagó por todo el jardín:

. . . . . .

Era un acorde lamento
de juventud y de amor

. . . . . .

"El jardín tiene una fuente
y la fuente una quimera. . . ."
Cantaba una voz doliente,
alma de la primavera.

Calló la voz y el violín
apagó su melodía.
Quedó la melancolía
vagando por el jardín.
Sólo la fuente se oía.

11. "In the middle of the plaza and on rough stone"

En medio de la plaza y sobre tosca piedra,
el agua brota y brota. En el cercano huerto
eleva, tras el muro ceñido por la hierda,
alto ciprés, la mancha de su ramaje yerto.

La tarde está cayendo frente a los caserones
de la ancha plaza en sueños. Relucen las vidrieras
con ecos mortecinos de sol. En los balcones
hay formas que parecen confusas calaveras.

La calma es infinita en la desierta plaza,
donde pasea el alma su traza de alma en pena.
El agua brota y brota en la marmórea taza.
En todo el aire en sombra no más que el agua suena.

12. "Where the poor river ends, the immense sea awaits"

"Donde acaba el pobre río la inmensa mar nos espera."

Bajo los ojos del puente pasaba el agua sombría.
(Yo pensaba: el alma mía.)

Y me detuve un momento,
en la tarde, a meditar. . . .
¿Qué es esta gota en el viento
que grita al mar: soy el mar?

13. "Every man has two / battles"

Todo hombre tiene dos
batallas que pelear.
En sueños lucha con Dios;
y despierto, con el mar.

14. "The soul conquers"

El alma vence. . . .

. . . . .

al ángel de la muerte y al agua del olvido.

Su fortaleza opone al tiempo, como el puente
al ímpetu del río sus pétreos tajamares;
bajo ella el tiempo lleva bramando su torrente,
sus aguas cenagosas huyendo hacia los mares.

15. "I know not what / divine poet"

Yo no sé qué noble,
divino poeta,
unió a la amargura
de la eterna rueda

la dulce armonía
del agua que sueña,
y vendó tus ojos
¡pobre mula vieja!

Más sé que fue un noble,
divino poeta,
corazón maduro
de sombra y de ciencia.

16. "Which is true?"

¿Cuál es la verdad? ¿El río
que fluye y pasa
donde el barco y el barquero
son también ondas del agua?
¿O este soñar del marino
siempre con ribera y ancla?

17. "I cannot chant, nor praise"

¡No puedo cantar, ni quiero
a ese Jesús de madero,
sino al que anduvo en el mar!

18. "Every man who journeys"

Todo el que camina anda,
como Jesús, sobre el mar.

19. "All things change"

Todo pasa y todo queda;
pero lo nuestro es pasar,
pasar haciendo caminos,
caminos sobre la mar.

20. "But though unto unknown sea it flows"

Pero aunque fluya hacia la mar ignota,
es la vida también agua de fuente
que. . . .
. . . . . .
. . . . sobre la piedra brota.
Y allí suena tu nombre ¡eternamente!

21. "Oh water good"

¡Oh agua buena, deja vida
en tu huida!
¡Oh tú, que vas gota a gota,
fuente a fuente y río a río,
como este tiempo de hastío
corriendo a la mar remota
con cuanto quiere nacer,
cuanto espera
florecer
al sol, de primavera,
sé piadosa,
que mañana
serás espiga temprana,
prado verde, carne rosa,
y más: razón y locura
y amargura
de querer y no poder
creer, creer y creer.

22. "Traveler, your footsteps are / the road"

Caminante, son tus huellas
el camino, y nada más;
caminante, no hay camino,
se hace camino al andar.
Al andar se hace camino,
y al volver la vista atrás
se ve la senda que nunca
se ha de volver a pisar.
Caminante, no hay camino,
sino estelas en la mar.

23. "I, on roads of afternoon, go / dreaming"

Yo voy soñando caminos
de la tarde, ¡Las colinas
doradas, los verdes pinos,
las polvorientas encinas! . . .
¿Adónde el camino irá?
Yo voy cantando, viajero
a lo largo del sendero . . .
—La tarde cayendo está—.
"En el corazón tenía
la espina de una pasión;
logré arrancármela un día,
ya no siento el corazón.

Y todo el campo un momento
se queda, mudo y sombrío,
meditando. Suena el viento
en los álamos del río.
La tarde más se obscurece;
y el camino que serpea
y débilmente blanquea,
se enturbia y desaparece.

Mi cantar vuelve a plañir:
"Aguda espina dorada,
quien te pudiera sentir
en el corazón clavada."

24. "Over the bitter earth"

Sobre la tierra amarga,
caminos tiene el sueño
laberínticos, sendas tortuosas,
parques en flor y en sombra y en silencio;

criptas hondas, escalas sobre estrellas;
retablos de esperanzas y recuerdos.
Figurillas que pasan y sonríen
—juguetes melancólicos de viejo—;

imágenes amigas,
a la vuelta florida del sendero,
y quimeras rosadas
que hacen camino . . . lejos. . . .

25. "The red sun of a dream"

El rojo sol de un sueño en el Oriente asoma.
Luz en sueños. ¿No tiemblas, andante peregrino?
Pasado el llano verde, en la florida loma,
acaso está el cercano final de tu camino.

26. "Oh, chambers of time and galleries / of the soul"

¡Oh cámeras del tiempo y galerías
del alma! ¡tan desnudas!
dijo el poeta. De los claros días
pasan las sombras mudas.

Se apaga el canto de las viejas horas
cual rezo de alegrías enclaustradas;
el tiempo lleva un desfilar de auroras
con séquito de estrellas empañadas.
¿Un mundo muere? ¿Nace
un mundo? ¿En la marina
panza del globo hace
nueva nave su estela diamantina?
¿Quillas al sol la vieja flota yace?
¿Es el mundo nacido en el pecado,
el mundo del trabajo y la fatiga?
¿Un mundo bueno para ser salvado
otra vez? ¡Otra vez! Que Dios lo diga.
Calló el poeta, el hombre solitario,
porque un aire de cielo aterecido
le amortecía el fino estradivario.
Sangrábale el oído.
Desde la cumbre vio el desierto llano
con sombras de gigantes con escudos,
y en el verde fragor del oceano
torsos de esclavos jadear desnudos.
Y un nihil de fuego escrito
tras de las selva huraña
en áspero granito,
y el rayo de un camino en la montaña . . .

27. "It is a bright afternoon"

. . . . Es una tarde clara,
casi de primavera,

. . . . . .

y estoy solo, en el patio silencioso,
buscando una ilusión cándida y vieja:
alguna sombra sobre el blanco muro,
algún recuerdo, en el pretil de piedra
de la fuente dormida. . . . .

. . . . . .

En el ambiente de la tarde flota
ese aroma de ausencia,
que dice al alma luminosa: nunca,
y al corazón: espera.

28. "Then as a flame"

Brotó como una llama la luz de los cabellos
que él en sus madrigales llamaba rubias olas,
brotó, porque una aroma igual tuvieron ellos . . .
Y se alejó en silencio para llorar a solas.

29. "The land is bare"

Desnuda está la tierra,
y el alma aúlla al horizonte pálido
como loba famélica. ¿Qué buscas,
poeta, en el ocaso?

Algunos yertos árboles negrean;
en los montes lejanos
hay oro y sangre . . . El sol murió . . . ¿Qué buscas,
poeta, en el ocaso?

30. "In the afternoon which broad as boredom is and clear"

En una tarde clara y amplia como el hastío,
cuando su lanza blande el tórrido verano,
copiaban el fastasma de un grave sueño mío,
mil sombras en teoría, enhiestas sobre el llano.

La gloria del ocaso era un purpúreo espejo,
era un cristal de llamas, que al infinito viejo
iba arrojando el grave soñar en la llanura . . .
Y yo sentí la espuela sonora de mi paso
repercutir lejana en el sangriento ocaso,
y más allá, la alegre canción de un alba pura.

31. "Last night as I slept"

Anoche, cuando dormía
soñé, ¡bendita ilusión!,
que una fontana fluía
dentro de mi corazón.

Di: ¿por qué acequia escondida,
agua, vienes hasta mí,
manantial de nueva vida
en donde nunca bebí?

Anoche cuando dormía
soñé, ¡bendita ilusión!,
que una colmena tenía
dentro de mi corazón;
y las doradas abejas
iban fabricando en él
con las amarguras viejas,
blanca cera y dulce miel.

Anoche cuando dormía
soñé, ¡bendita ilusión!,
que un ardiente sol lucía
dentro de mi corazón.

Era ardiente porque daba
calores de rojo hogar,
y era sol porque alumbraba
y porque hacía llorar.

Anoche cuando dormía
soñé, ¡bendita ilusión!,
que era Dios lo que tenía
dentro de mi corazón.

32. "How often have you erased"

¡Cuántas veces me borraste,
tierra de ceniza,
estos limonares verdes
con sombras de tus encinas!

33. "Water is good as is our thirst"

Buena es el agua y la sed;
buena es la sombra y el sol;
la miel de flor de romero,
la miel de campo sin flor.

34. "And then he saw his sacred muse"

Y vio la musa esquiva,
de pie junto de su lecho, la enlutada,
la dama de sus calles, fugitiva,
la imposible al amor y siempre amada.
Díjole Abel: Señora,
por ansia de tu cara descubierta,
he pensado vivir hacia la aurora
hasta sentir mi sangre casi yerta.
Hoy sé que no eres tú quien yo creía;
mas te quiero mirar y agradecerte
lo mucho que me hiciste compañía
con tu frío desdén.
Quiso la muerte
sonreir a Martín, y no sabía.

35. "And must sun from new day erased be?"

¿Y ha de borrarse el sol del nuevo día?
Abel tendió su mano
hacia la luz bermeja
de una caliente aurora de verano,
ya en el balcón de su morada vieja.

Ciego, pidió la luz que no veía.
Luego llevó, sereno,
el limpio vaso, hasta su boca fría,
de pura sombra—¡oh, pura sombra!—lleno.

36. "To die . . ."

Morir . . . ¿Caer como gota
de mar en el mar inmenso?
¿O ser lo que nunca he sido:
uno, sin sombra y sin sueño,
un solitario que avanza
sin camino y sin espejo?

37. "The trees have / green leaves still"

Los árboles conservan
verdes aún las copas,
pero del verde mustio
de las marchitas frondas.

. . . . .

Arrastra el viento algunas
amarillentas hojas.

38. "While pass the shadows of a holy love"

Mientras la sombra pasa de un santo amor, hoy quiero
poner un dulce salmo sobre mi viejo atril.
Acordaré las notas del órgano severo
al suspirar fragante del pífano de abril.

Madurarán su aroma las pomas otoñales,
la mirra y el incienso salmodiarán su olor;
exhalarán su fresco perfume los rosales,
bajo la paz en sombra del tibio huerto en flor.

Al grave acorde lento de música y aroma,
la sola y vieja y noble razón de mi rezar
levantará su vuelo suave de paloma,
y la palabra blanca se elevará al altar.

39. "The land of Soria arid is and cold"

I

Es la tierra de Soria árida y fría.
Por las colinas y las sierras calvas,
verdes pradillos, cerros cenicientos,
la primavera pasa
dejando entre las hierbas olorosas
sus diminutas margaritas blancas.

La tierra no revive, el campo sueña.
Al empezar abril está nevada
la espalda del Moncayo:
el caminante lleva en su bufanda
envueltos cuello y boca, y los pastores
pasan cubiertos con sus luengas capas.

II

La tierras labrantías,
como retazos de estameñas pardas,
el huertecillo, el abejar, los trozos
de verde obscuro en que el merino pasta,
entre plomizos peñascales, siembran
el sueño alegre de infantil Arcadia.

En los chopos lejanos del camino,
parecen humear las yertas ramas
como un glauco vapor—las nuevas hojas—,
y en las quiebras de valle y barrancas
blanquean los zarzales florecidos
y brotan las violetas perfumadas.

40. "The spring has come"

La primavera ha venida,
¡Aleluyas blancas
de los zarzales floridos!

41. "Spring gently the tree grove kissed"

La primavera besaba
suavemente la arboleda,
y un verde nuevo brotaba
como una verde humareda.

Las nubes iban pasando
sobre el campo juvenil . . .
Yo vi en las hojas temblando
las frescas lluvias de abril.

Bajo ese almendro florido,
todo cargado de flor,
—recordé—, yo he maldecido
mi juventud sin amor.

Hoy, en mitad de la vida,
me he parado a meditar . . .
¡Juventud nunca vivida,
quién te volviera a soñar!

42. "Aware only of my chimera"

Como atento no más a mi quimera
no reparaba en torno mío, un día
me sorprendió la fértil primavera
que en todo el ancho campo sonreía.

Brotaban verdes hojas
de las hinchadas yemas del ramaje,
y flores amarillas, blancas, rojas,
alegraban la mancha del paisaje.

Y era una lluvia de saetas de oro
el sol sobre las frondas juveniles;
del amplio río en el caudal sonoro
se miraban los álamos gentiles.

Tras de tanto camino es la primera
vez que miro brotar la primavera,
dije, y después, declaratoriamente:

—¡Cuán tarde ya para la dicha mía!—
y luego, al caminar, como quien siente
alas de otra ilusión:—Y todavía
¡yo alcanzaré mi juventud un día!

43. "Love's poplars that yesterday held / nightingales"

¡Álamos de amor que ayer tuvisteis
de ruiseñores vuestras ramas llenas;
álamos que seréis mañana liras
del viento perfumado en primavera!

44. "In your old tree a young song you wear"

En tu árbol viejo anida un canto adolescente,
del ruiseñor de antaño la dulce melodía.
Poeta, que declaras arrugas en tu frente,
tu musa es la más noble: se llama Todavía.

. . . . .

Poeta, el alma sólo es ancla en la ribera,
dardo cruel y doble escudo adamantino;
y en el diciembre helado, rosal de primavera;
y sol del caminante y sombra del camino.

Poeta, que declaras arrugas en tu frente,
tu noble verso sea más joven cada día;
que en tu árbol viejo suene el canto adolescente,
del ruiseñor eterno la dulce melodía.

45. "In these endless / galleries of memory"

En esas galerías
sin fondo del recuerdo
donde las pobres gentes
colgaron cual trofeo

el traje de una fiesta
apolillado y viejo,
allí el poeta sabe
el laborar eterno
mirar de las doradas
abejas de los sueños.

Poetas con el alma
atenta al hondo cielo,
en la cruel batalla
o en el tranquilo huerto,

la nueva miel labramos
con los dolores viejos,
la veste blanca y pura
pacientemente hacemos,
y bajo el sol bruñimos
el fuerte arnés de hierro.

46. "Man in thought"

Cabeza meditadora,
¡qué lejos se oye el zumbido
de la abeja libadora!

Echaste un velo de sombra
sobre el bello mundo, y vas
creyendo ver, porque mides
la sombra con un compás.

Mientras la abeja fabrica,
melifica,
con jugo de campo y sol,
yo voy echando verdades
que nada son, vanidades
al fondo de mi crisol.
De la mar al percepto,
del percepto al concepto,
del concepto a la idea
—¡oh, la linda tarea!—
de la idea a la mar.
¡Y otra vez a empezar!

47. "On the elm old"

Al olmo viejo, hendido por el rayo
y en su mitad podrido,
con las lluvias de abril y el sol de mayo
algunas hojas verdes le han salido.

¡El olmo centenario en la colina
que lame el Duero! Un musgo amarillento
le mancha la corteza blanquecina
al tronco carcomido y polvoriento.

No será, cual los álamos cantores
que guardan el camino y la ribera,
habitado de pardos ruiseñores.

Ejército de hormigas en hilera
va trepando por él y en sus entrañas
urden sus telas grises las arañas.

Antes que te derribe, olmo del Duero,
con tu hacha el leñador, y el carpintero
te convierta en melena de campana,
lanza de carro y yugo de carreta;
antes que rojo en el hogar, mañana,
ardas, de alguna mísera caseta,
al borde de un camino,
antes que te descuaje un torbellino
y tronche el soplo de las sierras blancas;
antes que el río hasta la mar te empuje
por valles y barrancas,
olmo, quiero anotar en mi cartera
la gracia de tu rama verdecida.
Mi corazón espera
también, hacia la luz y hacia la vida,
otro milagro de la primavera.

48. "As the snow melts"

Al borrarse la nieve, se alejaron
los montes de la sierra.
La vega ha verdecido
al sol de abril, la vega
tiene la verde llama,
la vida, que no pesa;
y piensa el alma en una mariposa,
atlas del munda, y sueña.
Con el circuelo en flor y el campo verde,
con el glauco vapor de la ribera,
en torno a las ramas,
con las primeras zarzas que blanquean,
con este dulce soplo
que triunfa de la muerte y de la piedra,
esta amargura que me ahoga fluye
en esperanza de Ella . . .

49. "Palacio, dear friend"

Palacio, buen amigo,
¿está la primavera
vistiendo ya las ramas de los chopos
del río y los caminos? En la estepa
del alto Duero, primavera tarda,
¡pero es tan bella y dulce cuando llega! . . .
¿Tienen los viejos olmos
algunas hojas nuevas?
Aún las acacias estarán desnudas
y nevados los montes de las sierras.
¡Oh, mole del Moncayo blanca y rosa,
allá en el cielo de Aragón, tan bella!
¿Hay zarzas florecidas
entre la fina hierba?
Por esos campanarios
ya habrán ido llegando las cigueñas.
Habrá trigales verdes,
y mulas pardas en las sementeras,
y labriegos que siembran los tardíos
con las lluvias de abril. Ya las abejas
libarán del tomillo y el romero.
¿Hay ciruelos en flor? ¿Quedan violetas?
Furtivos cazadores, los reclamos
de la perdiz bajo las capas luengas,
no faltarán. Palacio, buen amigo,
¿tienen ya ruiseñores las riberas?
Con los primeros lirios
y las primeras rosas de las huertas,
en una tarde azul, sube al Espino,
al alto Espino donde está su tierra.

50. "It matters not that golden wine / should lie"

Y nada importa ya que el vino de oro
rebose de tu copa cristalina,
o el agrio zumo enturbie el puro vaso . . .

Tú sabes las secretas galerías
del alma, los caminos de los sueños,
y la tarde tranquila
donde van a morir. . . . Allí te aguardan

las hadas silenciosas de la vida,
y hacia un jardín de eterna primavera
te llevarán un día.

The Dialogue With Time

51. "Amid the high plains"

Los sueños dialogados

I

¡Cómo en el alto llano tu figura
se me parece! . . . Mi palabra evoca
el prado verde y la árida llanura,
la zarza en flor, la cenicienta roca.

Y al recuerdo obediente, negra encina
brota en el cerro, baja el chopo al río;
el pastor va subiendo a la colina;
brilla un balcón de la ciudad: el mío,

el nuestro. ¿Ves? Hacia Aragón, lejana,
la sierra de Moncayo, blanca y rosa . . .
Mira el incendio de esa nube grana,

y aquella estrella en el azul, esposa.
Tras el Duero, la loma de Santana
se amorata en la tarde silenciosa.

II

¿Por qué, decísme, hacia los altos llanos,
huye mi corazón de esta ribera,
y en tierra labradora y marinera
suspiro por los yermos castellanos?

Nadie elige su amor. Llevóme un día
mi destino a los grises calvijares
donde ahuyenta al caer la nieve fría
las sombras de los muertos encinares.

De aquel trozo de España, alto y roquero,
hoy traigo a ti, Guadalquivir florido,
una mata del áspero romero.

Mi corazón está donde ha nacido,
no a la vida, al amor, cerca del Duero . . .
¡El muro blanco y el ciprés erguido.

III

Las ascuas de un crepúsculo, señora,
rota la parda nube de tormenta,
han pintado en la roca cenicienta
de lueñe cerro un resplandor de aurora.

Una aurora cuajada en roca fría,
que es asombro y pavor del caminante
más que fiero león en claro día,
o en garganta de monte osa gigante.

Con el incendio de un amor, prendido
al turbio sueño de esperanza y miedo,
yo voy hacia la mar, hacia el olvido

—y no como a la noche ese roquedo,
al girar del planeta ensombrecido—.
No me llaméis, porque volver no puedo.

IV

¡Oh, soledad, mi sola compañía,
oh musa del portento, que el vocablo
diste a mi voz que nunca te pedía!,
responde a mi pregunta: ¿con quién hablo?

Ausente de ruidosa mascarada,
divierto mi tristeza sin amigo,
contigo, dueña de la faz velada,
siempre velada al dialogar conmigo.

Hoy pienso: este que soy será quien sea;
no es ya mi grave enigma este semblante
que en el íntimo espejo se recrea,

sino el misterio de tu voz amante.
Descúbreme tu rostro, que yo vea
fijos en mí tus ojos de diamante.

52. "Always steadfast, never changed"

Siempre firme, siempre igual
impasible, casta y buena,
¡Oh tú, robusta y serena
eterna encina rural

. . . . .

y tú, encinar madrileño,

. . . . .

con tu adustez castellana
corrigiendo
la vanidad y el atuendo
y la hetiquez cortesana.

53. "The evil man abounds in field and town"

Abunda el hombre malo del campo y de la aldea,
capaz de insanos vicios y crímenes bestiales,
que bajo el pardo sayo esconde un alma fea,
esclava de los siete pecados capitales.

54. "Spain of brass bands and tambourines"

La España de charanga y pandereta,
cerrada y sacristía,
devota de *Frascuelo* y de María
. . . . . que ora y embiste,
cuando se digna usar de la cabeza.

55. "Soria, cold land, Soria pure"

¡Soria fría, *Soria pura,*
cabeza de Extremadura,
con su castillo guerrero
arruinado, sobre el Duero;
con sus murallas roídas
y sus casas denegridas!

Muerta ciudad de señores,
soldados o cazadores;
de portales con escudos
de cien linajes hidalgos,
y de famélicos galgos,
de galgos flacos y agudos,
que pululan
por las sórdidas callejas,
y a medianoche ululan,
cuando graznan las cornejas!

¡Soria fría! La campana
de la Audiencia da la una.
Soria ciudad castellana,
¡tan bella! bajo la luna.

56. "This man is neither of yesterday nor of a future day"

Este hombre no es de ayer ni es de mañana,
sino de nunca; de la cepa hispana
no es el fruto maduro ni podrido,
es una fruta vana
de aquella España que pasó y no ha sido,
ésa que hoy tiene la cabeza cana.

57. "It was a day in mid-July."

A orillas del Duero

Mediaba el mes de julio. Era un hermoso día.
Yo, solo, por las quiebras del pedregal subía,
buscando los recodos de sombra, lentamente.
A trechos me paraba para enjugar mi frente
y dar algún respiro al pecho jadeante;
o bien, ahincando el paso, el cuerpo hacia adelante
y hacia la mano diestra vencido y apoyado
en un bastón, a guisa de pastoril cayado,
trepaba por los cerros que habitan las rapaces
aves de altura, hollando las hierbas montaraces
de fuerte olor—romero, tomillo, salvia, espliego—.
Sobre los agrios campos caía un sol de fuego.

Un buitre de anchas alas, con majestuoso vuelo,
cruzaba solitario el puro azul del cielo.
Yo divisaba, lejos, un monte alto y agudo,
y una redonda loma cual recamado escudo,
y cárdenas alcores sobre la parda tierra
—harapos esparcidos de un viejo arnés de guerra—

las serrezuelas calvas por donde tuerce el Duero
para formar la corva ballesta de un arquero
en torno a Soria.—Soria es una barbacana
hacia Aragón que tiene la torre castellana—.
Veía el horizonte cerrado por colinas
obscuras, coronadas de robles y de encinas;
desnudas peñascales, algún humilde prado
donde el merino pace y el toro arrodillado
sobre la hierba rumia, las márgenes del río
lucir sus verdes álamos al claro sol de estío,
y silenciosamente, lejanos pasajeros,
¡tan diminutos!—carros, jinetes y arrieros—
cruzar el largo puente y bajo las arcadas
de piedra ensombrecerse las aguas plateadas
del Duero.

El Duero cruza el corazón de roble
de Iberia y de Castilla.

¡Oh, tierra triste y noble,
la de los altos llanos y yermos y roquedas,
de campos sin arados, regatos ni arboledas;
decrépitas ciudades, caminos sin mesones,
y atónitos palurdos sin danzas ni canciones
que aún van, abandonando el mortecino hogar,
como tus largos ríos, Castilla, hacia la mar!

Castilla miserable, ayer dominadora,
envuelta en sus andrajos desprecia cuanto ignora.
¿Espera, duerme o sueña? ¿La sangre derramada
recuerda, cuando tuvo la fiebre de la espada?
Todo se mueve, fluye, discurre, corre o gira;
cambien la mar y el monte y el ojo que los mira.
¿Pasó? Sobre sus campos aún el fantasma yerra
de un pueblo que ponía a Dios sobre la guerra.

La madre en otro tiempo fecunda en capitanes
madrasta es hoy apenas de humildes ganapanes.
Castilla no es aquella tan generosa un día
cuando Mío Cid Rodrigo el de Vivar volvía,
ufano de su nueva fortuna y su opulencia,
a regalar a Alfonso los huertos de Valencia;
o que, tras la aventura que acreditó sus bríos,
pedía la conquista de los inmensos ríos
indianos a la corte, la madre de soldados,
guerreros y adalides que han de tornar cargados
de plata o oro a España, en regios galeones,
para la presa cuervos, para la lid leones.
Filósofos nutridos de sopa de convento
contemplan impasibles el amplio firmanento;
y si les llega en sueños, como un rumor distante,
clamor de mercadores de muelles de Levante,
no acudirán siquiera a preguntar ¿qué pasa?
Y ya la guerra ha abierto las puertas de su casa.

Castilla miserable, ayer dominadora,
envuelta en sus harapos desprecia cuanto ignora.

El sol va declinando. De la ciudad lejana
me llega un armonioso tañido de campana
—ya irán a su rosario las enlutadas viejas—.
De entre las peñas salen dos lindas comadrejas;
me miran y se alejan, huyendo, y aparecen
de nuevo, ¡tan curiosas! . . . Los campos se obscurecen.
Hacia el camino blanco está el mesón abierto
al campo ensombrecido y al pedregal desierto.

58. "The blood of Cain" (Selections from "La tierra de Alvargonzález)

Mucha sangre de Caín
tiene la gente labriega,

. . . . .

La condicia de los campos
ve tras la muerte la herencia.

. . . . . .

Martín que estaba en la huerta
cavando . . .

. . . . . .

. . . tenía
la sangre de horror helada.
La azada que hundió en la tierra
teñida de sangre estaba.

. . . . . .

Dióse a trabajar la tierra
con fe y tesón el indiano,

. . . . . .

Ya con macizas espigas,
preñadas de rubios granos,
a los campos de Miguel
tornó el fecundo verano.

59. "Tell me, martial plane"

Di tú, avión marcial, si el alto Duero
a donde vas recuerda a su poeta,

. . . .

¿o es, otra vez, Caín, sobre el planeta,
bajo tus alas, moscardón guerrero?

60. "Spirits of cowardice and hate run loose"

Manes de odio y de la cobardía
cortan la leña de tus encinares,
pisan la baya de oro en tus lagares,
muelen el grano que tu suelo cría.

61. "And yet another Spain is being born"

Mas otra España nace,
le España del cincel y de la maza,
con esa eterna juventud que se hace
del pasado macizo de la raza.

62. "There is a Spaniard"

Ya un español que quiere
vivir y a vivir empieza,
entre una España que muere
y otra España que bosteza.
Españolito que vienes
al mundo, te guarde Dios.
Una de las dos Españas
ha de helarte el corazón.

63. "In depth of all our dreams"

Ya entonces por el fondo de nuestro sueño—herencia
de un siglo que vencido sin gloria se alejaba—
un alba entrar quería; con nuestra turbulencia
la luz de las divinas ideas batallaba.

Mas cada cual el rumbo siguió de su locura;
agilitó su brazo, acreditó su brío;
dejó como un espejo bruñido su armadura
y dijo: "El hoy es malo, pero el mañana . . . es mío."

Y es hoy aquel mañana de ayer . . . Y España toda,
con sucios oropeles de Carnaval vestida
aún la tenemos: pobre y escuálida y beoda;
mas hoy de un vino malo: la sangre de su herida.

Tú, juventud más joven, si de más alta cumbre
la voluntad te llega, irás a tu aventura
despierta y transparente a la divina lumbre:
como el diamante clara, como el diamante pura.

64. "With the melancholy of your word"

Con ese libro de melancolía,
toda Castilla a mi rincón me llega;
Castilla la gentil y bravía;
la parda y la manchega.
¡Castilla, España de los largo ríos
que el mar no ha visto y corre hacia los mares;
Castilla de los páramos sombríos,
Castilla de los negros encinares!

. . . . . .

. . . . . . Azorín, yo creo
en el alma sutil de tu Castilla,

. . . . . .

Desde un pueblo que ayuna y se divierte,

. . . . . .

creo en la libertad y en la esperanza,
y en una fe que nace
cuando se busca a Dios y no se alcanza,
y en el Dios que se lleva y se hace.

. . . . . .

¡Oh, tú, Azorín, escucha! España quiere
surgir, brotar, toda una España empieza!
¿Y ha de helarse en la España que se muere?
¿Ha de ahogarse en la España que bosteza?
Para salvar la nueva epifanía
hay que acudir, ya es hora,
con el hacha y el fuego al nuevo día.
Oye cantar los gallos de la aurora.

65. "Since the master now is gone"

Como se fue el maestro,
la luz de esta mañana
me dijo: Van tres días
que mi hermano Francisco no trabaja.
¿Murió? . . . Sólo sabemos
que se nos fue por una senda clara,
diciéndonos: Hacedme
un duelo de labores y esperanzas.
Sed buenos y no más, sed lo que he sido
entre vosotros: alma.
Vivid, la vida sigue,
los muertos mueren y las sombras pasan;
lleva quien deja y vive el que ha vivido.
¡Yunques, sonad; enmudeced, campanas!

Y hacia otra luz más pura
partió el hermano de la luz del alba,
del sol de los talleres,
el viejo alegre de la vida santa.
. . . ¡Oh, sí!, llevad, amigos,
su cuerpo a la montaña,
a los azules montes
del ancho Guadarrama.
Allí hay barrancos hondos
de pinos verdes donde el viento canta.
Su corazón repose
bajo una encina casta,
en tierra de tomillo, donde juegan
mariposas doradas . . .
Allí el maestro un día
soñaba un nuevo florecer de España.

Notes

The Generation of 1898: An Introduction

1. Angel Ganivet y García (1865-1898), Miguel de Unamuno y Jugo (1964-1936), Ramón María del Valle-Inclán (1869-1936), Antonio Machado y Ruiz (1875-1939), Pío Baroja y Nessi (1872-1956) and José Martínez Ruiz, called Azorín (1873-1967).

2. Pío Baroja, *Memorias* (Madrid: Taurus, 1955), p. 1235. See also the chapter on "The National Aspect of Temporality."

3. Vetusta is the vaguely disguised city of Oviedo in Alas' novel *La regenta* (Madrid: Alianza Editorial, 1967), p. 7.

4. Leopoldo Alas, *Obras selectas* (Madrid: Plenitud, 1947), p. 817.

5. Manual and Antonio Machado. *Obras completas*. 3rd edition. (Madrid: Editorial Plenitud, 1957), p. 833. All references to Machado's works, unless otherwise indicated, are taken from this edition and will be identified in subsequent notes by page number only. All italics in quotations, unless otherwise indicated, are mine.

6. For additional recent studies on Galdós in particular as well as his relationship with the Generation of '98, the reader is directed to Joaquín Casalduero, *Vida y obra de Galdós* (Buenos Aires, 1943); Sherman H. Eoff, *The Novels of Pérez Galdós: The Concept of Life as Dynamic Process* (Saint Louis, 1954); Germán Beilberg and E. Inman Fox (eds.), *Spanish Thought and Letters in the Twentieth Century* (Nashville, 1966); and the bibliographies included in these volumes especially articles by Casalduero, Gustavo Correa, H. Chonon Berkowitz, Theodore A. Sackett and Joseph Schraibman.

7. Liverpool Institute of Hispanic Studies monograph series; also published as F. Courtney Tarr, "Romanticism: A Symposium, Spain," *PMLA* (1925), pp. 35-46, 59-60.

8. José de Espronceda (1808-1842) was a lyric poet influenced by the English romantics, creator of a don Juan figure called Félix de Montemar and the only Spanish romantic with a world view, as expressed in the incomplete *El diablo mundo* (The Devil World). Gustavo Adolfo Bécquer (1836-1870), a latter-day romantic, was both lyric poet and author of legends; he was influenced by Hoffman and Heine. Mariano José de Larra (1809-1837) was an embittered, agonized and extremely modern essayist and critic.

9. José Martínez Ruiz (Azorín), *Las confesiones de un pequeño filósofo,* in the series *Obras Completas* (Madrid; Aguilar, 1947), II, 43.

10. Miguel de Unamuno, *Del sentimiento trágico de la vida* in *Ensayos* (Madrid: Aguilar, 1958), II, 836.

11. Angel Ganivet, *La cofradía del Avellano* (Granada, n.d.), p. 101. This is a collection of Ganivet's letters compiled by Nicholás María López.

12. Ganivet, *Los trabajos del infatigable creador, Pío Cid* in *Obras Completas* (Madrid: Aguilar, 1951), II, 9-10. Hereafter this novel will be referred to as *Los trabajos* and his first novel about Pío Cid, *La conquista del reino de Maya por el último conquistador español, Pío Cid,* as *La conquista.*

13. The biographical problem of Guiomar's identity is discussed in footnote 10 of the chapter "Images and Cycles."

14. Doris King Arjona, "*Voluntad* and *Abulia* in Contemporary Spanish Literature," *Revue Hispanique,* LXXIV (1928), 640ff.

15. See particularly for additional recent material on Ganivet the centenary issue of *Papeles de Son Armadans* XL (March, 1966).

16. The *Idearium español* has been translated as *Spain: An Interpretation.* The word "idearium" is Ganivet's invention and untranslatable. As an *aviarium* is a place where one would find birds (*aves*) and a *lapidarium,* stones (*lapides*), so an *idearium* would house ideas.

17. Ganivet, *Las trabajos, Obras,* II, 449.

18. Ganivet, *Idearium español* (Madrid: Espasa-Calpe, 1954), p. 98.

19. *Ibid.,* p. 13.

20. Ganivet, *La conquista, Obras*, I, 648.
21. Ganivet, *Idearium*, p. 10.
22. Ganivet, *Los trabajos, Obras*, II, 440.
23. *Ibid.*, pp. 76-77.
24. Ganivet, "Las ruinas de Granada," *Obras*, II, 718.
25. Unamuno, *Del sentimiento trágico de la vida, Ensayos*, II, 771-772. Throughout the text this essay is referred to as the *Tragic Sense.*
26. *Ibid.*, p. 735.
27. *Ibid.*, pp. 769-770.
28. Unamuno, *La vida de don Quijote y Sancho*, in *Obras Selectas* (Madrid: Plenitud, n.d.), p. 359.
29. Unamuno, "Mi religión," *Obras*, p. 257.
30. Unamuno, *Abel Sánchez, Obras*, pp. 751-834.
31. Unamuno, *San Manuel Bueno, mártir*, OBRAS, p. 1128.
32. *Ibid.*, p. 1140.
33. Unamuno, *Tragic Sense, Ensayos*, II, 1022.
34. Pedro Laín Entralgo, *España como problema* (Madrid: Aguilar, 1957), pp. 354-657.
35. Ramón María del Valle-Inclán, *Obras completas* (Madrid: Aguilar, 1954), II, 1892.
36. Valle-Inclán, *Sonata de invierno* (winter) in *Sonatas* (Madrid: Plenitud, 1957), p. 621. There is a sonata for each of the other seasons: *Sonata de primavera* (spring), *Sonata de estío* (summer) and *Sonata de otoño* (autumn).
37. Leon Livingston, "The Pursuit of Form in the Novels of Azorín," *PMLA*, LXXVI (1962), 116-133.
38. Azorín, *El escritor* (Madrid: Espasa-Calpe, 1957), p. 46.
39. *Ibid.*, p. 65.
40. Azorín, *Las confesiones de un pequeño filósofo* in *Obras Completas* (Madrid: Aguilar, 1957), II, 37.
41. Literally *actual* means *present*; hence *inactual* would mean *not of the present.*
42. Azorín, *Las confesiones de un pequeño filósofo*, OBRAS, II, 54-55.
43. Azorín, *El caballero inactual*, p. 93.
44. Azorín, OBRAS, II, 243.
45. Leon Livingston, "The Pursuit of Form in the Novels of Azorín," *PMLA* LXXVI (1962), 125.

46. Azorín, *La voluntad*, OBRAS, I, 888.

47. Anna Krause, *Azorín, The Little Philosopher* (Berkeley: University of California Press, 1948), p. 237.

48. Leon Livingston, "The Pursuit of Form . . .," p. 131.

49. Angel Valbuena Prat, *Historia de literatura española* (Barcelona: Gili Gaya, 1960), III, 497.

50. Leon Livingston, "The Pursuit of Form . . .," p. 133.

51. Azorín, *El caballero inactual*, pp. 135-136.

52. The three parts of *La lucha por la vida* were published in 1904, *Paradox, rey* in 1906 and *El árbol de la ciencia* (hereafter referred to as *El árbol*) in 1911.

53. Enrique Anderson-Imbert, *Veinte cuentos españoles del siglo XX* (Twenty Twentieth Century Spanish Stories), New York, 1961, p. 43.

54. Baroja, *El árbol* in *Obras Completas* (Madrid: Biblioteca Nueva, 1947), II, 569.

55. P. 915.

56. P. 855.

57. Pp. 911-912.

58. P. 649.

59. In the play *La Lola se va a los puertos* the heroine is based upon Guiomar.

60. See primarily José Luis Cano's several articles in the identity of Guiomar as well as biographies by McVan and Pérez Ferrero cited in the bibliography.

61. Machado's works, frequently recompiled and reanthologized, incude: *Soledades* (1903), *Soledades, galerías y otros poemas* (1907), *Humorismos, fantasías, apuntes* (n.d.), *Campos de Castilla* (1912, revised 1919), *Nuevas canciones* (1924), *De un cancionero apócrifo* (parts of which appeared in 1926 in the magazine *Revista de Occidente*, the compete volume having been published in 1933), miscellaneous prose work and some poetry written during the Civil War which has never been included in the Spanish edition of the complete works. These last poems as well as the final prose pieces were originally published in the magazine *Hora de España.*

62. Alice Jane McVan, *Antonio Machado* (New York: Hispanic Society of America, 1959), pp. 87-88.

63. Hugh Thomas, *The Spanish Civil War* (New York: Harper and Row, 1961), p. 608.

Nature as an Expression of Temporality

1. P. 783 (from "La Tierra de Alvargonzález").
2. P. 1016.
3. P. 1017.
4. P. 1016.
5. P. 1075.
6. P. 1099.
7. *Hora de España,* XIII (June, 1938), 8.
8. P. 924.
9. P. 846.
10. Azorín, *La voluntad,* p. 77.
11. P. 847.
12. P. 718.
13. P. 1042.
14. See the discussion below of the poem "Sobre la tierra amarga," in the chapter Images and Cycles.
15. Pp. 716-717.
16. P. 1006.

Images and Cycles

1. Unamuno, *Tragic Sense,* pp. 758-759.
2. P. 803.
3. Pp. 748-749.
4. P. 660.
5. P. 728.
6. *Ibid.*
7. P. 939.
8. *Ibid.*
9. P. 940.
10. Recently identified as Pilar de Valderrama, Machado's Guiomar had long been the subject of conflicting opinions, considerable investigation and great expenditure of ink. The publication in 1950, in most unscholarly circumstances, of letters purportedly from Machado to Guiomar added more controversy rather than illumination to the matter. The reality of Guiomar in no sense authenticates all of the letters nor justifies the aura of romantic sentimentality in which

their appearance was wrapped (Concha Espina, *De Antonio Machado a su grande y secreto amor*, Madrid: Lifesa, 1950). Several details of the correspondence—particularly concerning noctural visits by the lady, resident in Madrid, to Machado in Segovia—defy verification. Since absence, distance from the beloved, is an essential quality of love and is often so described in the Guiomar poems, the attitude of the poems is difficult to reconcile with a literal interpretation of the letters. The discovery of the correspondence remains inadequate documentation for the "great and secret love." Indeed before the fact of a poet who celebrates "la hora de una cita *imaginaria*" (the appointed hour of an imaginary meeting), the question of how large a role the imagination played in the supposed romance is still far from answered.

11. P. 984.
12. Pp. 655-656.
13. Pp. 658-659.
14. Pp. 856-857.
15. P. 727.
16. Carlos Bousoño, *Teoría de la expresión poética* (Madrid: Gredos, 1956), p. 137.
17. P. 822.
18. P. 664.
19. Pp. 825-826.
20. Unamuno, *Tragic Sense*, p. 759.
21. P. 1143. "Man would not have invented the clock if he did not believe in death. The clock is, in effect, an indirect proof of man's belief in his mortality, for only finite time can be measured."
22. Unamuno, *Tragic Sense*, p. 735.
23. P. 853.
24. Pp. 691-692.
25. P. 904.
26. Pierre Damangeat, "Machado: Poet of Solitude," *Cronos*, II (March, 1948), 53.
27. P. 808.
28. See above: references such as "where the poor river ends the immense sea awaits."
29. P. 820.
30. P. 740.
31. P. 830.

32. P. 929.
33. P. 803.
34. "What is the most terrible aspect of death? Simply to die or the thought of continuing to live, as now, blindly? . . . But there is yet another possibility, that of not merely preserving our personality but of finding it." (Baeza, 1915) in *Cartas inéditas de Antonio Machado*, ed. Manuel García Blanco, *Revista Hispánica Moderna*, XXII (1956), 273.
35. P. 830.
36. P. 678.
37. P. 826.
38. P. 651.
39. The knowledge gained from his traveling is an understanding of the people he has seen: "Everywhere I have seen caravans of grief . . ." etc.
40. P. 915. The poem is addressed to Ramón María del Valle-Inclán.
41. P. 661.
42. See below, discussion of images of afternoon.
43. P. 671.
44. See above, p. 64.
45. P. 720.
46. P. 989.
47. Gerardo Diego, "*Tempo lento* en Antonio Machado," *Cuadernos Hispanoamericanos*, Nos. 11-12 (1949), pp. 421-426.
48. P. 1087.
49. Bousoño, *Teoría de la expresión poética*, p. 167.
50. Julián Marías, "Antonio Machado y su interpretación poética de las cosas," *Cuadernos Hispanoamericanos*, Nos. 11-12 (1949), pp. 307-321.
51. The first edition of *Soledades* (Madrid: A. Alvarez) bears the date 1903 but actually appeared in the last months of 1902 (McVan, *Antonio Machado*, p. 18). Machado first published in the magazine *Electra* in 1901 when he was twenty-six.
52. Azorín's belief that: "things constitute the frontier of man."
53. P. 806.
54. P. 760.
55. P. 802.
56. P. 718.

57. P. 657.
58. P. 695.
59. Pp. 717-718.
60. Pp. 666-667.
61. P. 724.
62. P. 973.
63. P. 704.
64. P. 891.
65. P. 886.
66. P. 895.
67. See above, p. 78.
68. P. 876.
69. P. 792.
70. Pp. 888-889.
71. Pp. 987-988 ("Muerte de Abel Martín," part III).
72. Pp. 988-989 ("Muerte de Abel Martín," part V).
73. Segundo Serrano Poncela, *Antonio Machado: su mundo y su obra* (Buenos Aires: Editorial Losada, 1954), pp. 130-135.
74. *Ibid.*
75. Baeza, 1913. In "Cartas inéditas," p. 106.
76. *Ibid.*, p. 273.
77. Pp. 830-831.
78. Juan de Mairena in *Hora de España,* XIII (January, 1938), 11.
79. P. 798.
80. P. 807.
81. P. 793.
82. P. 749.
83. P. 750.
84. P. 724.
85. P. 670.
86. P. 757.
87. P. 759.
88. P. 879.
89. P. 939.
90. P. 660.
91. P. 721.
92. P. 1076.
93. P. 695.

94. P. 761.
95. Pp. 852-854.
96. Unamuno, *Tragic Sense*, p. 736.
97. Pp. 706-707.
98. P. 704.
99. P. 837.
100. P. 748.
101. P. 720.
102. P. 677.
103. "Cartas inéditas," p. 106.
104. Pp. 789-790.
105. P. 796.
106. Pp. 798-799.
107. P. 731.
108. P. 795.
109. P. 713.

The Dialogue with Time

1. P. 824.
2. Pp. 923-924.
3. Pp. 938-939. "The Five Forms of Objectivity Studied by Abel Martín," also mentioned in "Unedited Works," pp. 1186-1187.
4. P. 966.
5. P. 936.
6. P. 1158.

Spain: The National Aspect of Temporality

1. Baroja, *Juventud egolatría* (Madrid: 1920), pp. 71-72.
2. Manuel García Viño, "El paisaje poético de Antonio Machado," *Archivo Hispalense*, XXIV (1956), 259-273.
3. P. 962. With Mairena we would add "in anticipation of facile objections—that the poetic talent of Góngora and the robust genius of Quevedo, Gracían and Calderón are as evident as the aesthetic inanity of culturalism and conceptualism."

4. Laín Entralgo, *España como problema,* pp. 355-368 and *passim.*
5. Pp. 746-747.
6. P. 761.
7. P. 741.
8. P. 756.
9. P. 741.
10. P. 746.
11. P. 854.
12. Unamuno, "La crisis del patriotismo," *Ensayos,* I, 287.
13. P. 737.
14. "Cartas inéditas," p. 103.
15. Letter to Unamuno, written in Madrid, September 24, 1921 and quoted in OBRAS, pp. 1239-1240.
16. Undated letter to Guiomar, quoted by Concha Espina (*Antonio Machado a su grande y secreto amor*), p. 112.
17. McVan, *Antonio Machado*, pp. 39-41.
18. P. 818.
19. Serrano Poncela, *Antonio Machado: su mundo y su obra*, pp. 157-187 and Laín Entralgo, *España como problema*, p. 457.
20. See above, p. 73.
21. Pp. 818, 809, 832.
22. P. 760. Machado's italics.
23. P. 809.
24. Pp. 734-736.
25. Ramón Menéndez Pidal, *Historia de España* (Madrid, 1947), I, ixxl-cl.
26. P. 654.
27. Pp. 762-788. "La tierra de Alvargonzález" was first published as a short story in *Mundial Magazine* in 1912. The entire prose text has been reprinted in Helen Grant's comparative study of the two versions, *Celtiberia,* III (1953), 57-90.
28. Allen W. Phillips, "La tierra de Alvargonzález: verso y prosa," *Nueva Revista de Filología Hispánica,* IX (1955), 131-132.
29. *Hora de España,* XIII (June, 1938), 6.
30. *Ibid.*, p. 9.
31. P. 819.
32. P. 833.
33. P. 847.

34. Pp. 808-809 and 818-819 respectively.
35. Pp. 843-846.
36. See the poem "Otro clima," discussed above, p. 73.
37. Pp. 839-840.

Conclusion

1. Pp. 116-117. Machado's italics.
2. W. H. Auden, *The Enchafèd Flood* (New York: Vintage Books, 1967), pp. 12, 43-44, 50, 81 and 87.
3. Northrop Frye, *Anatomy of Criticism* (New York: Atheneum, 1968), p. 105.
4. P. 952.
5. P. 1157.

A Selected Bibliography

THIS LIST cites, besides the editions of Machado's works used, the most important critical sources consulted during preparation of the manuscript. Several of the books mentioned have extensive bibliographies and these have been indicated below. Inasmuch as this study is not dependent upon other critical works or articles, I have avoided attempting either a complete or a critical bibliography. The works listed would be excellent points of departure for those desiring to read more about Machado.

Primary Sources

Machado y Ruiz, (Manuel y) Antonio. *Obras completas.* 3rd ed. Madrid: Editorial Plenitud, 1957. This is not a complete edition, not only because Machado chose to omit some of his early work from later collections but also because poems composed during the Spanish Civil War and published in *Hora de España* have been intentionally overlooked.

————. Verso. *Hora de España.* XIII (June, 1938), 5-11.

————. "Miscelanea apócrifa." *Hora de España.* XIII (January, 1938) 7-16, (February) 5-10, (March) 5-11, (April) 5-10, (May 5-9, (July) 5-12, (August) 5-12, (September) 5-15 and (October) 9-15.

————. "Cartas inéditas de Antonio Machado a Unamuno," ed. Manuel García Blanco. *Revista Hispánica Moderna,* XXII (April and July-October, 1956), 97-114 and 270-285.

————. "Cartas de Antonio Machado a Juan Ramón Jiménez." *La Torre*, VII, No. XXV, 159-196.

Secondary Sources

Albornoz, Aurora de. *Poesías de guerra de Antonio Machado*. San Juan de Puerto Rico: Ediciones Asomante, 1961.

————. "La presencia de Segovia en Antonio Machado," *Ínsula*, XIX (1964), ccxii-ccxiii, pp. 9-10.

Allen, Rupert C. "Un poema existencialista de Antonio Machado," *Duquesne Hispanic Review*, II (1963), pp. 1-71.

————. "Structure in the poetry of Antonio Machado," unpublished dissertation, University of California, Berkeley, 1960.

Alonso, Dámaso. *Cuatro poetas españoles*. Madrid: Gredos, 1958.

Aranguren, José Luis. "Esperanza y desesperanza de Dios en la experiencia de Antonio Machado," *Cuadernos Hispanoamericanos*, Nos. 11-12 (1949), pp. 383-397.

Auden, W. H. *The Enchafèd Flood*. New York: Vintage Books, 1967.

Barja, César. *Literatura española: libros y autores contemporáneos*. New York: Stechert, 1935.

Bell, Aubrey Fitzgerald. *Contemporary Spanish Literature*. New York: Knopf, 1933.

Bo, Carlos. "Observaciones sobre Antonio Machado," *Cuadernos Hispanoamericanos*, Nos. 11-12 (1949), pp. 523-539.

Bousoño, Carlos. *Teoría de la expresión poética*. Madrid: Gredos, 1956.

Cano, José Luis. "Antonio Machado, hombre y poeta en sueños," *Cuadernos Hispanoamericanos*, Nos. 11-12 (1949), pp. 653-665.

————. "Un soneto de Machado a Guiomar," *Quaderni-Iberoamericani*, No. 26, pp. 71-73.

Carbonell, Reyes. "Más notas estilísticas sobre la poesía de Antonio Machado," *Duquesne Hispanic Review*, I (1962), pp. 11-23.

Carpintero, Heliodoro. "Historia y poesía de Antonio Machado," *Celtiberia*, Nos. 2 (1951), pp. 307-356.

————. "Soria en la vida y en la obra de Antonio Machado," *Escorial*, VII (1943), pp. 11-127.

Clavería, Carlos. "Notas sobre la poesía de Antonio Machado," *Hispania*, XXVII (1945), pp. 166-183.

Damangeat, Pierre, "Machado: Poet of Solitude," *Cronos*, II (1948), pp. 51-63.

Diego, Gerardo. "*Tempo lento* en Antonio Machado," *Cuadernos Hispanoamericanos*, Nos. 11-12 (1949), pp. 421-455.

Durán, Manuel. "Unamuno y Machado por dentro," *Revista Hispánica Moderna*, XXVIII (1961), pp. 39-41.

Espina, Concha. *De Antonio Machado a su grande y secreto amor.* Madrid: Lifesa, 1950.

Franco Oppenheimer, Félix. "El tema de la angustia en la poesía de Antonio Machado," *Alma Latina*, Nos. 786 and 787 (1950).

Frye, Northrop. *Anatomy of Criticism.* New York: Atheneum, 1968.

García Viño, Manuel. "El paisaje poético de Antonio Machado," *Archivo Hispalense*, XXIV (1956), pp. 259-273.

Gicovante, Bernardo. "Reflexiones en torno a 'La tierra de Alvargonzález,' " *Hispanófila*, No. 11 (1961), pp. 47-51.

————. "El testamento poético de Antonio Machado," *PMLA*, LXXI, pp. 42-50.

Grant, Helen F. "La tierra de Alvargonzález," *Celtiberia*, III (1953), pp. 57-90.

Guillén, Claudio. "Estilística del silencio," *Revista Hispánica Moderna*, XXIII, pp. 260-291.

Gullón, Ricardo. "Lenguaje, humanismo y tiempo en Antonio Machado," *Cuadernos Hispanoamericanos*, Nos. 11-12 (1949), pp. 567-581.

————. *Relaciones entre Antonio Machado y Juan Ramón Jiménez.* Pisa: University of Pisa, 1964.

————. "Unidad en la obra de Antonio Machado," *Insula*, IV 1949), p. 1.

Laín Entralgo, Pedro. *España como problema.* Madrid: Aguilar, 1957.

López-Morillas, Juan. "Antonio Machado's Temporal Interpretation of Poetry," *Journal of Aesthetics and Art Criticism*, VI (1947), pp. 161-171.

Machado, José. Carta, *Romance* I (1940), No. 3, p. 17.

McVan, Alice Jane. *Antonio Machado.* New York: Hispanic Society of America, 1959. Bibliography.

Marías, Julián. "Antonio Machado y su interpretación poética de las cosas," *Cuadernos Hispanoamericanos*, Nos. 11-12 (1949), pp. 307-321.

Morales, Rafael. "Andalucía y el tiempo a través de los versos de Antonio Machado," *El Español* (1944).

Morrow, Carolyn. "An analysis of 'Poema de un día': The Philosophy of Bergson in Machado's Concept of Time," *Romance Notes*, II, pp. 149-153.

Pérez Ferrero, Miguel. *Vida de Antonio y Manuel.* Madrid: Espasa-Calpe, 1952.

Phillips, Allen W. "La tierra de Alvargonzález: verso y prosa," *Nueva Revista de Filología Hispánica*, IX (1955), pp. 129-148.

Pradal-Rodríguez, Gabriel. "Antonio Machado: vida y obra," *Revista Hispánica Moderna*, XV (1949), pp. 1-80. Bibliography.

Predmore, Richard L. "El tiempo en la poesía de Antonio Machado," *Hispania*, XXIX, pp. 500-506.

Ribbans, Geoffrey, "Antonio Machado's *Soledades*: A Critical Study," *Hispanic Review*, XXX, pp. 194-215.

Rosales, Luis. "Muerte y resurrección de Antonio Machado," *Cuadernos Hispanoamericanos*, Nos. 11-12 (1949), pp. 435-479.

Ruiz de Conde, Justina. "¿Por qué la llamó Machado Guiomar?" *La Torre*, VIII (1960), pp. 61-72.

Ruiz Ramón, Francisco. "El tema del camino en la poesía de Antonio Machado," *Cuadernos Hispanoamericanos*, L, pp. 52-76.

Sánchez Barbudo, Antonio. *Estudios sobre Unamuno y Machado.* Madrid: Editorial Guadarrama, 1959.

————. "El pensamiento de Abel Martín y Juan de Mairena en relación con la poesía de Antonio Machado," *Hispanic Review*, XXII (1954), pp. 32-74 and 109-165.

Schwartz, Kessel. "The Sea and Machado," *Hispania*, XLVIII (1965), pp. 247-254.

Serrano Poncela, Segundo. *Antonio Machado: su mundo y su obra.* Buenos Aires: Editorial Losada, 1954.

Valverde, José María. "Evolución del sentido español de la obra de Antonio Machado," *Cuadernos Hispanoamericanos*, Nos. 11-12 (1949), pp. 399-414.

Zubiría, Ramón de. *La poesía de Antonio Machado.* Madrid: Gredos, 1955.

Index to Poems

Spanish Text

English Translation

Index